T0193518

THE GREATEST
PLEAS EVER MADE

PAUL E. ORMAN

WESTBOW
PRESS®
A DIVISION OF THOMAS NELSON
& ZONDERVAN

WestBow Press books may be ordered through booksellers or by contacting:

WestBow Press
A Division of Thomas Nelson & Zondervan
1663 Liberty Drive
Bloomington, IN 47403
www.westbowpress.com
844-714-3454

Scripture quotations are from the Holy Bible, King James Version (Authorized Version). First published in 1611. Quoted from the KJV Classic Reference Bible, Copyright © 1983 by The Zondervan Corporation.

ISBN: 978-1-6642-9406-6 (sc)
ISBN: 978-1-6642-9407-3 (hc)
ISBN: 978-1-6642-9408-0 (e)

Library of Congress Control Number: 2023904065

Print information available on the last page.

WestBow Press rev. date: 11/03/2023

Like most authors, I would like to take a brief opportunity to dedicate this work to those who have contributed greatly to my life. And at the top of that list are my parents, Donald and Nancy Orman. While my parents provided a wealth of material comfort, fun, family values, and safety during my childhood, the greatest thing they provided in *training up a child in the way he should go* (see Proverbs 22:6) was a solid spiritual foundation.

I was abundantly blessed to have been exposed to, what I consider to be, some of the greatest teachers and preachers of God's word within our country during my lifetime. At my birth, my parents were members of Merritt Island Baptist Church under Dr. Adrian Rodgers. My parents insisted that my sisters and I were in church for every service held. During my school years I had the honor to be pastored by Dr. Joseph Boatwright and mentored by Reverend Mitch White. I also benefitted from exposure to Dr. Jim Henry at First Baptist Church of Orlando.

Upon leaving home after enlisting in the U.S. Coast Guard, I sought out First Baptist Church of Ft. Lauderdale under Dr. OS Hawkins where I was also greatly influenced by Reverend Woody Cumbie. I had my first opportunity to preach under Dr. Darrell Orman at Miami Gardens Baptist Church. As a young adult, I sat under Dr. Scott Fenton in Plano Texas and spent a number of Thursday lunches at Prestonwood Baptist Church listening to the teachings of Zig Ziglar.

After I married my wife of twenty-six years, we spent several years in Richmond Virginia where we attended Grove Avenue Baptist Church with both Dr. Vander Warner, Jr. and Dr. Mark Beckton.

Time and time again, God provided strong, sound, and educational biblical teaching in my life that greatly influenced my interest and study habits of the Holy Bible. None of these would have been so impactful were it not for the foundation my parents laid so many years before. And for that, I will ever be grateful.

CONTENTS

A CRY FOR HELP?

Have you ever heard a cry for help? And I do not mean a question like "Could you please help me do the dishes?" I mean a sincere plea from someone who is in grave danger and who doesn't have any time to wait. Someone who needs help immediately, in the then and now, and whose life hangs in the balance. Few people will ever hear that desperate, blood curdling cry for help from someone whose life is in immediate danger with only seconds remaining. But if we were the person to hear that cry, it is very likely that we would want to respond.

The response to a cry for help is important. Someone who answers the call to help with the dishes might say "Be there in a minute," and while the person needing the help might be a little annoyed at the less-than-enthusiastic reply, there is great doubt that some grave calamity may befall the world if the help to do the dishes arrives a couple of minutes later than when it was asked for.

But consider someone who has just been involved in an accident and is injured to the point of having only moments to live. The cry for help is urgent. It is panicked. It is nondiscriminatory. And it is desperate. This kind of cry for help cannot tolerate "Be there in a minute," a minute would more than likely be about fifty-nine seconds too late. This cry demands a response, and it demands it right now. And if a response is not given, then all hope is lost, and the grip of fear tightens.

I served in the United States Coast Guard when I was younger, and one of my duties was to stand Radio Watch. Multiple US Coast Guard service men and women are constantly sitting at dedicated radio stations up and down the coast lines of our nation, intently listening for calls for help; they are there twenty-four hours a day, seven days a week, fifty-two weeks a year, year after year. They are there for the citizens of our country and all others within our territorial waters who find themselves in trouble or in need of assistance on the high seas.

During my time of service, I heard many calls of "Mayday! Mayday! Mayday!". Every single one of them, that I experienced, was different. In some I could distinguish the urgency in the voice of the caller. Some callers conveyed no urgency at all. And, of course, there were always those whose calls did not quite match the perceived urgency of the situation, such as those whose Mayday calls were calm and collected even though their vessels were on fire, or those whose calls were panicked and hysterical while they were sitting in their vessels anchored in calm waters, surrounded by other boats, and within wading distance of shore.

What was interesting about the calls for help was not necessarily the people in need, but the service men and women who responded. When a call from someone in need was received, some discernment on the part of the team who was responding to that call was required. If the danger was perceived to be great, the Duty Officer may have chosen to send a more experienced crew to assist. If there were several vessels involved, the Duty Officer may have been required to notify senior officers of the response. And if the danger was broad enough and grave enough, multiple units, or even multiple agencies might respond, all of which required on-scene coordination. There were escalating responses to increasingly critical situations and more desperate cries for help.

That was just in my experience. There are many other first responders around the world who are there, ready and listening for calls for help. Firefighters, police personnel, emergency medical technicians, and many others are dealing with calls for help constantly. Every day of every week, of every year of our lives there are calls for help. Some sources have cited that as many as 240 million 9-1-1 calls are made in the United States every single year. The United States population is about 331 million people (as of 2020), so the call statistics mean that one call for help is made by seventy percent of the population every year. That's a lot of calls for help. These statistics do not include the calls for help from boats and aircraft made to organizations such as the US Coast Guard, Air Traffic Control System, or the Civil Air Patrol. Neither do they include calls intercepted by military bases that have their own police, fire, and emergency medical services.

Granted, all these statistics include repeat callers. They include those whose emergencies do not quite meet the urgency most reasonable people would ascribe to life-or-death situations. And they include multiple calls for the same emergency such as a large automobile accident on a major interstate or a large high-rise building fire in a major city. But at the end of the day, there are a lot of calls for help. And most of these calls for help are responded to.

When responding to a cry for help, most seasoned first responders prioritize their response. They go to where they are needed the most and where they are needed immediately. It is critical that the necessary services be brought to those who need them the most in the most expeditious manner possible.

However, this brings up the question of discernment. How do we know whose cry for help is the most important? How do we know who is in the most need at any given time? Even more critical to discernment is the question of those who are simply unable to cry out for help.

What about all the people who simply suffer in silence while unaware that one call for help would bring much needed relief? What of those people who sink to such depths of despair that they end up taking their own lives? We often talk about looking for *signs* in suicide victims, but very rarely do we interpret the *signs* as cries for help. People who do not, and cannot, make pleas for help need to be considered as well. And how would a potential suicide victim who is moments away from taking his or her own life stack up in priority against a person who has been mortally wounded, or a homeless person who is destined to die on the street within hours, or the person who has just eaten his or her last meal with no hope of ever being able to afford or find another one?

What are the greatest pleas ever made? And what is their significance to the rest of us? Well, I would like to share with you what I think are the greatest pleas ever made in all human history. I want to share what their importance is to everyone who is alive today or who is yet to be born into this world. And I want to share why I think these pleas are applicable to our lives today and how they can be instrumental in our understanding of our own helplessness and need to cry out to God for his love, mercy, and salvation.

THE PLEA OF CURIOSITY

I believe the first of the greatest cries for help ever made is the plea of curiosity. Curiosity is an intense eagerness to know or to learn. It involves inquiring and seeking. And generally, those who look for signs of distress within a group of people, will tell you to pay attention to the questions the people ask. How have they changed, and what are the underlying implications? People who are curious are at least willing to consider salvation, whether they know it or not. And people who are curious, and who do not get their curiosity answered, are likely to slip into despair. So, when we see a plea of curiosity within a person, we should respond to it immediately because it is a cry of a person in desperate need, and there may not be much time before he or she is lost to withdrawing inward, blocking out the rest of the world.

The plea of curiosity is made by those searching for answers intently. It is a desperation in their lives for closure to some horrific event or some great mystery. And the plea of curiosity can drive people to the brink of their very sanity. They will invest all, risk all, and give of their all, in order to have one burning question answered in their lives. And we have an example of this recorded in history.

This great plea of curiosity was made some two thousand years ago by a man named Nicodemus who was a ruler of the Jews. His story is recorded in the Bible, in the book of John, chapter 3.

> There was a man of the Pharisees, named Nicodemus, a ruler of the Jews: The same came to Jesus by night, and said unto him, Rabbi, we know that thou art a teacher come from God: for no man can do these miracles that thou doest, except God be with him. (John 3:1–2)

Nicodemus was a Pharisee, a member of one of the Jewish religious sects at the time who believed in the resurrection of the human body from the dead and the coming of a *Messiah*, a deliverer of the Jews who would bring peace to the world. Nicodemus would have to have been a learned individual to hold this position. And he was looked upon as a ruler, a member of the government of the day. Such a person would have little to fear, yet he did not seem particularly interested in others seeing him meet with Jesus by light of day, so he went to Him under the cover of darkness at night. Why would Nicodemus do this? I believe it was his burning curiosity that drove him to risk such an interaction.

Nicodemus was a person seeking answers. He was curious about the miracles he had witnessed, and he wanted to know more. He went to Jesus and told Him that he knew He must be a teacher come from God. And he reasoned this because no one could do the miracles that he had seen Jesus do, except that He be from God. Obviously, Nicodemus was missing some of the pieces of this puzzle, and he wanted to know more. He went to Jesus pleading that He would satisfy his curiosity.

> Jesus answered and said unto him, Verily, verily, I say unto thee, Except a man be born again, he cannot see the kingdom of God. Nicodemus saith unto him, How can a man be born when he is old? can he enter the second time into his mother's womb, and be born? Jesus answered, Verily, verily, I say unto thee, Except a man be born of water and of the Spirit, he cannot enter into the kingdom of God. That which is born of the flesh is flesh; and that which is born of the Spirit is spirit. Marvel not that I said unto thee, Ye must be born again. The wind bloweth where it listeth, and thou hearest the sound thereof, but canst not tell whence it cometh, and whither it goeth: so is every one that is born of the Spirit. (John 3:3–8)

Here is how we know it was a plea: Jesus answered him. Jesus believed that Nicodemus was pleading out of his curiosity because He provided him with an answer. And His answer was immediate and to the point. Notice that Jesus wanted to address Nicodemus's curiosity. He told him that in order to see the kingdom of God, he *must* be born again. And we learn why Nicodemus's original plea of curiosity makes sense. Nicodemus was coming to Jesus in the belief that He *had* to have come from God because only someone who had come from God could do the miracles the people had been watching Jesus perform. Nicodemus was seeking the kingdom of God; he was hoping that, if Jesus was come from God, He would show him the kingdom of God.

What a great plea! "Rabbi, Rabbi [or Teacher, Teacher], show me the kingdom of God!" What drove Nicodemus to come out that night, to meet with Jesus, to risk being seen associating with Jesus? It was the hope of seeing the kingdom of God.

Jesus showed great discernment in understanding why Nicodemus had come to Him and what he was seeking. We know He was exactly on point because of Nicodemus's reaction. Nicodemus did not respond with "What in the world are you talking about, Jesus?" or "No, you misunderstood me. That wasn't what I was asking." Nicodemus was immediately ready to carry on the conversation. Nicodemus's plea of curiosity was, "Yes, I want to see the kingdom of God, but I do not know how to accomplish what you are telling me."

Notice how Nicodemus responded. He took Jesus's answer seriously and said, "Wait a minute. How is that possible?" or "How does one do that?" And I know that Nicodemus was taking Jesus quite seriously because Nicodemus had already testified to the miracles; he had seen Jesus do, and he had concluded that only a teacher come from God could perform such miracles. So Nicodemus isn't about to dismiss lightly anything that Jesus said. And Jesus's answer drives his curiosity even further. I am sure that Nicodemus was saying, "Okay, if that is how I get to see the kingdom of God, then tell me more. How can someone be born again?"

And Jesus once again went directly to the heart of Nicodemus's plea of curiosity. Jesus immediately explains that He is not talking about a physical rebirth but rather a spiritual rebirth. Jesus told Nicodemus that the misunderstanding was that they were not talking about a physical rebirth of flesh and blood, but rather of a spiritual rebirth that is of one's spirit, that while one knows it is there—one sees and hears evidence of it—one cannot discern where it came from or where it will end up. But Nicodemus was still not connecting the dots.

Nicodemus answered and said unto him, How can these things be? Jesus answered and said unto him, Art thou a master of Israel, and knowest not these things? Verily, verily, I say unto thee, We speak that we do know, and testify that we have seen; and ye receive not our witness. If I have told you earthly things, and ye believe not, how shall ye believe, if I tell you of heavenly things? And no man hath ascended up to heaven, but he that came down from heaven, even the Son of man which is in heaven. And as Moses lifted up the serpent in the wilderness, even so must the Son of man be lifted up: That whosoever believeth in him should not perish, but have eternal life. For God so loved the world, that he gave his only begotten Son, that whosoever believeth in him should not perish, but have everlasting life. For God sent not his Son into the world to condemn the world; but that the world through him might be saved. He that believeth on him is not condemned: but he that believeth not is condemned already, because he hath not believed in the name of the only begotten Son of God. And this is the condemnation, that light is come into the world, and men loved darkness rather than light, because their deeds were evil. For every one that doeth evil hateth the light, neither cometh to the light, lest his deeds should be reproved. But he that doeth truth cometh to the light, that his deeds may be made manifest, that they are wrought in God. (John 3: 9–21)

Nicodemus cried out in one last desperate plea of curiosity, "How? Tell me how can these things be!" And that was where Jesus began to help Nicodemus understand all that he was seeking. And in the good fashion of helping those who help themselves, Jesus began by reminding Nicodemus who he was. Notice He reminded him that he was a *master of Israel*. Jesus was telling Nicodemus, "You know these things. You have studied these things. You are a master. You teach others." How many times do those with the plea of curiosity have the very answers they seek sitting right in front of them? If they would only slow down and observe what is already around them and what they already know, oftentimes they would have at least some of their curiosities satisfied. Jesus expertly answered Nicodemus's plea of curiosity by showing him how many of the answers he already had.

And then Jesus began to help Nicodemus connect the dots. Jesus told Nicodemus, "You've heard Me speak, you've seen the miracles, and yet you still do not believe. So, if you do not believe the earthly things, how in the world can you believe if I tell you of the heavenly things?" Jesus was helping Nicodemus understand that seeing the kingdom of God begins with belief—not just belief in things seen but belief in things unseen. It was a step of faith.

Jesus told Nicodemus that He knew he wanted to see the kingdom of God, but no person had ever ascended into the heavens and seen the kingdom of God, save one. And Jesus told Nicodemus that the one who had seen the kingdom of God, was the one who came down from the kingdom of God—the Son of man who was presently in heaven. Nicodemus would have understood perfectly at this point that Jesus was telling him "**I AM GOD**". Jesus would have been saying "Nicodemus, you are correct in saying I am from God. I am God come down from heaven." And then Jesus referenced Holy Scriptures that Nicodemus would have been familiar with and told Nicodemus that they were a foreshadowing of things to come.

We may wonder if, when Nicodemus saw Jesus hanging upon the cross, as he almost surely did, he would have remembered the night he went to Jesus and all that Jesus told him. It is at this point right here that Jesus answered Nicodemus's plea of curiosity.

> And as Moses lifted up the serpent in the wilderness,
> even so must the Son of man be lifted up: That whosoever
> believeth in him should not perish, but have eternal life.
> (John 3:14–15)

Jesus was saying, "Nicodemus, whoever believes in Jesus Christ will not perish, but will have eternal life, and will get to see the kingdom of God." Nicodemus, being a master of Israel, would have understood perfectly what Jesus was telling him. Nicodemus should have, and would have, come to the realization that God in the flesh stood before him and had come from heaven, the kingdom of God, to die.

And we know this because the *crime* that Jesus was charged with later, was that of claiming to be God. He was found to be blaspheming in the view of the Jewish religious leadership of the day. And indeed, at one point they attempted to stone him for such a claim (John 8:58–59). This was something that had been commanded by the law of Moses (Leviticus 24:16). However, just in case this was not a clear enough point to Nicodemus, Jesus reiterated his statement with some further clarification.

> For God so loved the world, that he gave his only begotten Son, that whosoever believeth in him should not perish, but have everlasting life. For God sent not his Son into the world to condemn the world; but that the world through him might be saved. He that believeth on him is not condemned: but he that believeth not is condemned already, because he hath not believed in the name of the only begotten Son of God. (John 3:16–18)

Jesus told Nicodemus that God loved the world so much that He gave up his only Son, whom Nicodemus would have recognized as Jesus referring to himself as the "Son of man," and that God gave Him up so that all those who believed in Him, would have everlasting life. And Nicodemus, being a Pharisee, the religious sect that believed in the resurrection of the dead, would have instantly equated this with seeing the kingdom of God, which was, after all, the curiosity that Jesus had identified when Nicodemus first came to Him.

Jesus added some clarification by saying that He had not come into the world to condemn, but rather to save. He told Nicodemus that belief in the Son would bring no condemnation in life, but that failure to believe would mean being already condemned, because not believing in the name of the only begotten Son of God left people in condemnation.

All of this would have made sense to Nicodemus. He would have understood that to see the kingdom of God, he would need to be free of condemnation; that is, he would need to be free of sin. To be free of his sin, he would need to be forgiven, because forgiveness releases people from condemnation. Sin, or failure to keep the Mosaic Law, would have been perfectly clear to Nicodemus, and he would have understood the condemnation of such an action. Nicodemus would have understood that Jesus was telling him the path to having his sins forgiven and being free of condemnation, was belief in the only begotten Son of God, whom Jesus had just told him was He that stood before him. Nicodemus would have now understood the spiritual rebirth that Jesus had talked about as the requirement for seeing the kingdom of God. The spiritual rebirth came about with belief in Jesus Christ. This is how Jesus ended his conversation with Nicodemus:

> And this is the condemnation, that light is come into the world, and men loved darkness rather than light, because their deeds were evil. For every one that doeth evil hateth the light, neither cometh to the light, lest his deeds should be reproved. But he that doeth truth cometh to the light, that his deeds may be made manifest, that they are wrought in God. (John 3: 19–21)

Jesus told Nicodemus that humankind knew of their condemnation because light had come into the world, but that the deeds of humankind were evil, and they loved darkness. Jesus was telling Nicodemus that God's light had exposed the evil—the sin—of humankind. And those who do evil hate the light because they are afraid their deeds may be reproved. But those who live in truth run to the light so that their deeds may be shown to be brought about by God. And perhaps Nicodemus may have understood that coming to the light, seeking truth, and stepping out of darkness, were the result of belief in the only begotten Son of God.

Did Nicodemus leave a changed person? We do not know for sure. This was the end of the recorded conversation. There are debates both ways as to whether Nicodemus ever believed in the only begotten Son of God. But what we do know for sure is that Jesus answered him directly and plainly about what was required to see the kingdom of God: Nicodemus, you must experience a spiritual rebirth, not of flesh, but in your spirit, and you accomplish that by believing in the only begotten Son of God, Jesus Christ, who came into the world to be lifted up on a cross and die so that the condemnation of your sin may be removed. Then you may see the kingdom of God.

This great plea was made at just the right time in history to recieve the greatest answer ever given.

The first greatest plea ever made: the plea of curiosity.

THE PLEA FOR MERCY

Sometimes people find themselves in circumstances completely outside of their control. Some circumstances are so overwhelming, it doesn't matter what people do or how they do it, they are still left helpless. People who are overwhelmed often feel trapped by their circumstances. And they feel there is nowhere for them to turn, nothing to grab hold of, and no ground to stand upon. And people who find themselves in this position cry out with pleas for mercy.

Mercy is relief in a person's life. It is an act of compassion and kindness that mitigates the circumstances in their lives. The plea for mercy is encouraged by unbearable situations that people are going through for which they have no answer and no solution.

The greatest plea for mercy in the history of the world was made by a certain man whose son was possessed by a demon, and we find the story recorded in the book of Matthew.

> And when they were come to the multitude, there came to him a certain man, kneeling down to him, and saying, Lord, have mercy on my son: for he is lunatick, and sore vexed: for ofttimes he falleth into the fire, and oft into the water. And I brought him to thy disciples, and they could not cure him. Then Jesus answered and said, O faithless and perverse generation, how long shall I be with you? how long shall I suffer you? bring him hither to me. And Jesus rebuked the devil; and he departed out of him: and the child was cured from that very hour. Then came the disciples to Jesus apart, and said, Why could not we cast him out? And Jesus said unto them,

> Because of your unbelief: for verily I say unto you, If ye
> have faith as a grain of mustard seed, ye shall say unto
> this mountain, Remove hence to yonder place; and it
> shall remove; and nothing shall be impossible unto you.
> (Matthew 17:14–20)

Note the very first thing that happened in this encounter with Jesus. Jesus and his disciples were approaching a multitude of people, a great crowd, and suddenly a man came out of the crowd and knelt before Jesus. Clearly this is a man who has exhausted all other resources and has nowhere else to turn. He comes and kneels before Jesus. Kneeling before a king or ruler was an act of recognizing the person's authority and one's own submission to that authority. This man knelt before Jesus in an act of submission; in doing so, he showed his total desperation.

Jesus was this man's last hope after he had lost all hope. The man pleaded for his son, "Lord, have mercy on my son." He knelt before Jesus and addressed him as Lord. And as he pleaded his case, he began to describe the calamities he had faced. His son often jumped into fire and at times into water, obviously putting his life in danger. And then others had to put their own lives in peril to save him from these dangers.

This certain man continued as he explained to Jesus just why his case was worthy to be heard by the Lord. He explained that he had tried every option available to him, including taking the child to Jesus's own disciples. And he must have had desperation in his voice as he exclaimed to Jesus that His own disciples had not been able to cure his son.

Just as it had been with Nicodemus, Jesus answered the certain man by going straight to the heart of his problem. Jesus immediately identified the problem as the man's association with a faithless and perverse generation. Jesus was saying that if a generation had faith and purity, they would not find such calamities in their midst and would not need to plead for mercy. Jesus addressed the cause that was bringing them to that moment in time—a faithless and perverse generation.

What Jesus said next may seem to be a complaint, but it was really an admonition to the people. When Jesus said, "how long shall I," what He was saying was "why do you not believe?" We will see this more clearly in the next chapter. Jesus was telling the certain man that He had been among the people for some time. And the people had seen many miracles from Him. Even Nicodemus had come to him in the dead of night and said that only a prophet from God could do what Jesus could do. And Jesus asked the people how much longer He needed to walk among them; and how much more He must show them before they began to have faith, before they began to believe, and before they began to turn from darkness to light. Jesus was saying, "How much more do I have to do before you understand and believe?"

Pleas for mercy are almost always a last resort for those who have lost all hope. They are generally from people who have lost faith in good outcomes to situations and no longer believe they can be saved. And Jesus reminded us here that, even when we believe there is no hope and that the circumstances are beyond our control, we are to continue in faith and purity.

And so, Jesus, recognized the situation for what it was and asked for the son to be brought before Him. And when the child was brought to Jesus, Jesus rebuked the demon inside of him, and the demon departed the child, and he was cured. According to the Bible, he was cured within the very same hour.

But then an interesting thing happens. We are told nothing further of the certain man who made the plea for mercy and we are told nothing further of his son who was cured. Certainly, the man's plea was answered, and he found mercy and grace; however, Matthew chose to tell us what happened with Jesus's disciples next.

> Then came the disciples to Jesus apart, and said, Why
> could not we cast him out? (Matthew 17:19)

The disciples took Jesus away from the crowd. Rather than immediately rejoicing in the child's cure, the answer to a plea for mercy, or a miracle, they wanted to focus on themselves and their own failures. I can just imagine the disciples witnessing Jesus cast the demon out of the child and thinking to themselves, *Wait a minute ..., we did exactly what Jesus did, just the way he taught us. Why didn't it work for us?*. This is a common occurrence among masters and students. Masters will oftentimes demonstrate skills in a craft, and when the students try to replicate the skill, they fall woefully short of success. Masters will generally then try to correct deficiencies in what is observed in the application of the student's abilities so that they can practice and become better. But I do not believe that is what happened here. Look at how Jesus answered them:

> And Jesus said unto them, Because of your unbelief: for verily I say unto you, If ye have faith as a grain of mustard seed, ye shall say unto this mountain, Remove hence to yonder place; and it shall remove; and nothing shall be impossible unto you. (Matthew 17:20)

Jesus did not tell them about a lack of proficiency in their skills; He did not provide them with a technique they needed to practice and perfect. Jesus didn't show them practice drills to run in order to make the team better for next season. In fact, Jesus did not say anything that would teach, instruct, or help the disciples improve their skills in casting out demons; rather Jesus directly identified a deficiency he saw in the disciples: unbelief. Jesus told the disciples that, if they wanted to cast out demons, they had better start with their own beliefs.

Jesus continued to emphasize His point by telling the disciples just how damaging unbelief can be. Notice that He told them that, even with the smallest amount of faith, they would be able to move mountains. He even told them that, with just a little faith, nothing would be impossible for them. However, unbelief can block faith. Jesus was telling the disciples, "It is not the size of your faith that matters here; it is the size of your unbelief." A little faith can go a long way, but unbelief will stop people short every single time.

As we read about Jesus telling His disciples of their shortcomings, we learn the greatest lesson and gain the greatest wisdom of all time: It is our unbelief that hinders us in life. It is our unbelief that causes us to fail. And it is our unbelief that keeps us from seeing the kingdom of God.

We would not have learned this lesson were it not for a plea for mercy. Why is a plea for mercy such a great plea? Well, I believe it is because it demonstrates that we have come to grips with ourselves. We recognize our own helplessness. We finally accept the fact that we are not in control and cannot save ourselves. It helps us understand and establish our belief and places our focus on Jesus.

We need more pleas for mercy in the world today. We need to all recognize that we are sinners and that we cannot help ourselves. We need to all recognize that we are helpless, hopeless, lost, drowning in sin and shame, and there is nothing we can do to control our situation. We need to come to the place in our lives where, like this certain man, we kneel at the feet of Jesus and plead for mercy—mercy from the Lord of all creation and mercy from the One who can show us the kingdom of God.

The second greatest plea ever made: The plea for mercy from the Lord.

THE PLEA FOR HELP
WITH UNBELIEF

The third greatest plea ever made was a plea for help. People oftentimes find themselves in positions of needing help. And while we all celebrate individual accomplishments, it is together that we reach for the stars. It is armies that win wars, not individual soldiers on their own. It is people who build great cities, not single engineers or craftspeople on their own. And it is great minds that come together to dream and to design and to build a spacecraft that will land humans safely on the moon and bring them home again, not a single rocket scientist on his or her own. People need other people, together they can accomplish great things.

But there are times when people find themselves in perilous situations and positions of imminent danger; for example, a position in which they know they are about to die. And it is at that moment in time when they realize they need help. They realize that they cannot get out of the peril that they find themselves in on their own. Others must provide them with some assistance.

I want to differentiate between the plea for mercy and the plea for help because they complement one another. The plea for mercy recognizes that there is nothing within your control that you can do to save yourself. You are totally reliant upon others to do everything for you in order that you can be saved. They are the ones in control, and they are the ones who have the power to either save you or to condemn you. The plea for help, on the other hand, implies that you require someone to come alongside you and assist you in the situation you find yourself in. You are still able to accomplish some things on your own, but you cannot do enough to save yourself.

Do you recall what Jesus said to Nicodemus in response to Nicodemus's plea of curiosity?

> He that believeth on him is not condemned: but he that believeth not is condemned already, because he hath not believed in the name of the only begotten Son of God. (John 3:18)

Jesus was saying that, while He was the only one who could save Nicodemus, there was still something required on his part: belief. We must believe in order to not be condemned. But if we do not believe in the name of the only begotten Son of God, we are condemned already.

And we all need both. We all need to recognize our helplessness and our need for mercy and grace, and at the same time recognize that we are required to believe and that we need help in our walk of faith.

So, knowing that, it should come as no surprise that the third greatest plea was made by the exact same person that made the second greatest plea. Makes sense, right? Because the plea for mercy and the plea for help go together.

But we are going to look at a slightly different account of the same story we looked at in the plea for mercy. In the plea for mercy, we saw the story unfold as Matthew recorded it. But now, in the plea for help, we are going to see the same story unfold as Mark recorded it.

> And one of the multitude answered and said, Master, I have brought unto thee my son, which hath a dumb spirit; And wheresoever he taketh him, he teareth him: and he foameth, and gnasheth with his teeth, and pineth away: and I spake to thy disciples that they should cast him out; and they could not. He answereth him, and saith, O faithless generation, how long shall I be with you? how long shall I suffer you? bring him unto me. And they brought him unto him: and when he saw him, straightway the spirit tare him; and he fell on the ground,

and wallowed foaming. And he asked his father, How long is it ago since this came unto him? And he said, Of a child. And ofttimes it hath cast him into the fire, and into the waters, to destroy him: but if thou canst do any thing, have compassion on us, and help us. Jesus said unto him, If thou canst believe, all things are possible to him that believeth. And straightway the father of the child cried out, and said with tears, Lord, I believe; help thou mine unbelief. When Jesus saw that the people came running together, he rebuked the foul spirit, saying unto him, Thou dumb and deaf spirit, I charge thee, come out of him, and enter no more into him And the spirit cried, and rent him sore, and came out of him: and he was as one dead; insomuch that many said, He is dead. But Jesus took him by the hand, and lifted him up; and he arose. (Mark 9:17–27)

So here we see the exact same story told from the perspective of a second person. We can see that the story has all the same elements; however, the level of detail is different. Mark chose to include some details that Matthew did not. And one detail crucial to us here is the second plea. The plea for help.

To begin with, Mark was not as focused on the plea for mercy as Matthew was. Notice how Mark began the story.

And one of the multitude answered and said, Master, I have brought unto thee my son, which hath a dumb spirit; And wheresoever he taketh him, he teareth him: and he foameth, and gnasheth with his teeth, and pineth away: and I spake to thy disciples that they should cast him out; and they could not. (Mark 9:17–18)

Mark did not tell us about the certain man kneeling before Jesus, or his pleading for mercy; however, he did provide a little more clarity to the situation. He included the information that the certain man told Jesus that his son did not talk, tore at himself, foamed at the mouth and gnashed his teeth. And if that wasn't bad enough, he refused to eat and was losing weight.

And we should note the phrase "he teareth him". Statistics among teenagers who self-mutilate (cut themselves) are hard to come by; however, some broad estimates figure as many as two to three million young adults in the United States repeatedly cut themselves with knives or razor blades each year.

Mark's account also includes the phrase "and pineth away". And while there are no clear statistics on anorexia and other eating disorders among young adults, some estimate that twenty million young adults in the United States suffer with such disorders.

I often wonder how many of these young adults who are plagued with cutting themselves and starving themselves; are being bullied by demons. We have a clear-cut example right here in Holy Scripture before us of a young man who was being terrorized by one of Satan's demons. The young man was cutting and starving himself. And we have similar cases in the world today, which we tend to dismiss as spiritual afflictions because of our unbelief. This is so ironic because; we, just like Jesus's disciples, are hindered in bringing help to people for the exact same reason: unbelief. I wonder how our own prayer lives would be changed should our unbelief be cured.

The next part of Mark's account is similar to Matthew's account up until the point when the son was brought before Jesus. At this point, Mark provides some additional dialogue between Jesus and the certain man.

> Jesus said unto him, If thou canst believe, all things
> are possible to him that believeth. (Mark 9:23)

Jesus came right back to the point of answering pleas: belief in the Son of God. Jesus told the certain man that his son could be saved, but success required belief. And He strengthened that claim with these words: "all things are possible to him that believeth." Jesus told the certain man that all things are possible. Of course his son could be saved, and it all started with belief in the Son of God. Here Mark records the certain man's second plea: the plea for help:

> And straightway the father of the child cried out, and
> said with tears, Lord, I believe; help thou mine unbelief.
> (Mark 9:24)

We see the father of the child immediately cry out. "Lord, I believe." Recall that the father was desperate at that point. He felt trapped. He felt helpless. His son had been tormented by a demon since his early youth. The man had tried everything including going to Jesus's disciples. This indicates that he had most likely also consulted doctors and the religious leaders of the day. He had probably made every appeal known to him, and finally, in his helplessness, he knelt before Jesus and pleaded for mercy. And Jesus told him "You have to believe." Jesus was saying, "You must believe in Me and that I have the power to save." So, of course, the man cried out, "Lord, I believe." Because he wanted to believe. He needed to believe. Belief was all he had left. But notice that he added something else: "Help thou mine unbelief."

And here we have the greatest plea for help ever made. I'd almost like to call it the forgotten plea for help. And I say 'forgotten' because people almost never, ever think to ask for help with their unbelief.

This certain man knelt before the Lord Jesus Christ, the only begotten Son of God. And he cried out "I believe." Yet he had the presence of mind to say to Jesus, "I need your help. Please help me with my unbelief." It is almost amazing to me that Jesus's disciples stood there and heard this conversation, witnessed these events, and then did not put two and two together to understand why they themselves had failed to cast out the demon.

This certain man had more insight and wisdom at that moment than Jesus's own disciples exhibited. And his insight and wisdom taught us that, while we may believe, it is still okay to ask for help with our unbelief.

People are very good at believing they have things handled. People also exhibit confidence when perhaps they should not. A lot of people around the world will tell you they believe in Jesus if you ask them. What they mean is they believe Jesus is a historical figure. They believe Jesus lived a couple of thousand years ago and that stories have been written about Him. They believe He was a very charismatic figure and may even acknowledge He has had an amazing impact on world history.

But what Jesus requires you to believe is that He is the Son of God and that God sent Him from heaven into a sinful world as the only sacrifice for sin. He requires that you believe He lived a sinless life while bringing God's message of salvation to the nation of Israel, and through them, to the world, and that, for His factual and truthful claim of being God in the flesh, He was wrongfully accused of blasphemy. You must believe that He was beaten and crucified on a cross and that He gave up His own life for you and for me and for all the world. You must believe that He was buried, and that on the third day, He arose and walked out of the tomb under His own power and that He ascended into heaven to be with God the Father and one day will return for His own.

And to believe all that takes some faith. So why wouldn't we ask for help in our unbelief? What an excellent lesson this certain man has taught us all: Lord, help me in my unbelief.

I am always wary when people tell me that they have a good relationship with the living God and that Jesus walks with them and talks with them. And then almost in the same breath, they tell me that they have trust issues. They have problems trusting those around them and the information they are given. These people need help with their unbelief.

The third greatest plea ever made: the plea for help with unbelief.

THE PLEA TO BE REMEMBERED

People want to be remembered. Some people strive to be immortalized in history forever. We need look no further than the social media platforms of our day to understand that people want to leave their marks. We build monuments to ourselves. We write our own histories. And we tell our stories to anyone who will listen. People just seem to have this built-in requirement to be remembered.

And this is so intriguing to me because I wonder if we ever stop to think about what that means or why it is so strong, especially to agnostics and atheists. Here in the United States, statues of historical figures have been removed in several cities in recent years. The names of entities named after historical figures have been changed. And it always amazes me because I do not think that one person has ever considered if the historical figure even cares. Does anyone really believe that Abraham Lincoln knew that there was some high school named after him in some American city? Of course he didn't. The high school wasn't named after him until after Lincoln had been dead for decades. And would he really care that we are now changing the name? Of course not. He's still dead.

So, what are people doing when they tear down these statues and rename schools and bridges? Are not they simply changing the dialogue of history? Because it is the ideals and beliefs of people that we want to remember. It is important to remember what they stood for and what they did. Some people who come along and do not like those ideals or beliefs want to then erase them from history and replace them with representations of their own ideals and beliefs. What is amusing to me is that these same people never seem to think that they are in the exact same boat. When they are dead and gone someone new will come along and want to tear down all that they have built and stood for and replace it with something different. And who will care then?

But there was one person in history whose plea to be remembered was answered correctly. Some two thousand years ago a thief on a cross made the greatest plea to be remembered ever made. And we find the account of this plea in Luke chapter 23.

> And when they were come to the place, which is called Calvary, there they crucified him, and the malefactors, one on the right hand, and the other on the left. Then said Jesus, Father, forgive them; for they know not what they do. And they parted his raiment, and cast lots. And the people stood beholding. And the rulers also with them derided him, saying, He saved others; let him save himself, if he be Christ, the chosen of God. And the soldiers also mocked him, coming to him, and offering him vinegar, And saying, If thou be the king of the Jews, save thyself. And a superscription also was written over him in letters of Greek, and Latin, and Hebrew, This Is The King Of The Jews. And one of the malefactors which were hanged railed on him, saying, If thou be Christ, save thyself and us. But the other answering rebuked him, saying, Dost not thou fear God, seeing thou art in the same condemnation? And we indeed justly; for we receive the due reward of our deeds: but this man hath done nothing amiss. And he said unto Jesus, Lord, remember me when thou comest into thy kingdom. And Jesus said unto him, Verily I say unto thee, Today shalt thou be with me in paradise. (Luke 23:33–43)

Here we find the story of the crucifixion of Jesus Christ. It is interesting to me that some two thousand years later, we still revere the symbol of the cross because it reminds us of Jesus's crucifixion. The name of a high school that honored former president Abraham Lincoln was disrespected after only a hundred years, but the cross of Jesus Christ has endured for an order of magnitude more and is still held up around the world today.

Luke tells us this story by saying that Jesus was brought to the place called Calvary, and that he was crucified there along with two malefactors, one on the right, and one on the left. And one might wonder about the significance of the two malefactors. Were they just recorded here for historical reference? And if that were the case, wouldn't we need a little more information about them in order to establish their significance and mark the point in history?

As it turns out, a very important event in history was about to take place involving these two malefactors and Luke didn't want us to miss it.

Luke continued by telling us that, as the three were crucified there at Calvary, Jesus asked the Father to forgive the crucifiers because they did not know what they were doing. And why wouldn't the people know what they were doing? I would suggest it was because of their unbelief. This is more than evident as, after they divided up Jesus's clothing and gambled over the garments, the religious rulers began to mock him. They suggested that, if he really was the Christ, the chosen of God, he should save himself. The soldiers also mocked him as the king of the Jews and taunted him to save himself and come down off the cross. And here we find that everything Jesus said earlier must happen, was happening, just as He described it would. And His only crime? The claim to be God. It was written in Greek and Latin and Hebrew on a sign hung over His head: "*This Is the King Of The Jews*". But these events prompted an interaction between the two thieves on either side of Him.

The first thief began to join in with the crowd in mocking Jesus. He echoed the crowd in saying "If thou be Christ, save thyself and us." This thief chose to use his last few hours alive, mocking the Son of God. The second thief, however, made a much wiser choice.

> But the other answering rebuked him, saying, Dost not thou fear God, seeing thou art in the same condemnation? And we indeed justly; for we receive the due reward of our deeds: but this man hath done nothing amiss And he said unto Jesus, Lord, remember me when thou comest into thy kingdom. (Luke 23:40–42)

Notice that he began with fear of God. What a great place from which to begin a plea. From a place of respect for the Lord. This thief was surprised that his fellow thief, would mock someone when he shared in the exact same fate. And oftentimes people find themselves in the same situation today. We find it easier to mock someone than to realize that we share the exact same fate with them.

The second thing this thief recognized is his own sin. He says, "And we indeed justly." He acknowledged that he deserved the punishment, that he was a sinner. Just like the first thief, people are very reluctant to recognize their own sin and admit that they deserve the death of the cross for their deeds. But how can we recognize that Jesus Christ took our place, paid our debt, and made it possible for us to see the kingdom of God, unless we first recognize that it should be us upon the cross in the first place?

The third thing the second thief recognized was the sinless nature of Jesus Christ. He says, "this man has done nothing amiss." Jesus had done nothing improper or wrong. In other words, this thief is saying "I find no fault in him." And we hear this repeatedly in the trial, death, and resurrection of Jesus Christ. He was without fault. He had committed no sin. And by recognizing the sinless nature of Jesus, this thief was recognizing the deity of Jesus Christ. This is such an important step for our world today in having our pleas heard. We need to recognize that Jesus Christ was God in the flesh.

Once the second thief expressed a fear of or respect for God, acknowledged his sin and that he deserved the punishment of the cross, and recognized the deity of Jesus Christ, he made his plea.

This was the fourth greatest plea ever made—the plea to be remembered. But the thief didn't just ask Jesus to remember him: he asked Jesus to remember him when He comes into His kingdom. And that is what makes this the fourth greatest plea of all time. Because, just like Nicodemus, this thief wanted to see the kingdom of God. And in order to do so, he placed all his faith and trust in Jesus Christ. He cried out "Lord! Remember me!" He had nowhere else to turn and no other hope left.

And Jesus said to him, "Today shalt thou be with me in paradise." And at that moment in time, the thief, whose name we do not even know, began a longer legacy than George Washington, Abraham Lincoln, or any other of America's founding fathers. And there are no monuments, no lengthy chapters in history books, no arguments in the streets over whether this thief should be remembered or not.

His place was already sealed, and he had seen the kingdom of God. On that day, he was with God in paradise. And all because he made the correct plea with the right spirit at the right time.

The fourth greatest plea ever made: the plea to be remembered by Jesus in His kingdom.

THE PLEA FOR HOPE

People need hope. Without hope, people give up and perish. Where there is no hope, there is despair. Hope is an easy thing to lose, and a difficult thing to acquire. And when people give up hope, they stop looking for salvation. Hope is vital to human existence.

So, why do people today not think through the consequences of their own beliefs? I have long contended that there are three basic world beliefs: Theists believe there is a god, Atheists believe there is no god. And Agnostics just take a wait-and-see approach without committing to any one belief or another. All the rest of our worldviews stem from one of these three base worldviews. Let's see how each of these base worldviews play out with hope for humanity.

People who have a theistic worldview, whether it be monotheistic or polytheistic, believe in something bigger than themselves that has a purpose for the world. There is a god with a plan. And perhaps that plan has something greater in store than just the physical world around us. The hope is that there is something more than just the existence that we now know. The hope extends to believing there is a rhyme and reason to all we see and experience, whether we understand it or not. The hope is that there is a real purpose in life.

People who have an atheistic worldview do not recognize a higher purpose. The world—indeed, the entire universe—is viewed as just all one big natural and explainable event. Is there any hope in this worldview? What does it matter? After all, atheists believe that we are only a product of natural forces and chance. It was simply an accident in time that created all that we see and experience around us. In this worldview; who cares if anyone is remembered or not? It is certain that, given enough time, all will be forgotten, and all accomplishments will be erased. If you are rich and die, what does it matter? Likewise, if you are poor and die, what does it matter? Everything is just atoms bumping into each other in the universe creating the illusion of order and purpose where there really is none. There is no hope with this worldview.

People who have an agnostic worldview make no commitment. And without commitment there can be no hope. For agnostiscs, if the atheist are correct their end is without hope. And if the theists are correct, because the agnostics failed to make a commitment and explore which god offered them hope, they still end with no hope. The agnostisc are like the lukewarm people that the Lord said He spews out of his mouth. Their lack of commitment condemns them already, and they are left without hope.

Some international polls find that about 51 percent of people believe in a god. And about 18 percent of people do not while 17 percent are undecided. Given any accuracy to these polls, only about half the people of the world population are theistic in their worldview; roughly the other half of the people are split between atheistic and agnostic. Is there any wonder then that the world lacks hope? A Gallop poll recently found that some 81 percent of Americans believe in a god.[1] I believe that people want to believe in a god because that sort of belief is designed into our beings. Our very nature—our makeup—is designed to make us want to believe in a god. This is independent of social or economic conditions and regardless of our upbringing or other experiences within our lives. This sort of belief drives hope. And this desire is there because it is vital to our very existence.

One of the greatest pleas that can be made in our lives is the plea for hope. Pleas for hope save lives as can be seen in this story:

> And the multitude rose up together against them: and the magistrates rent off their clothes, and commanded to beat them. And when they had laid many stripes upon them, they cast them into prison, charging the jailor to keep them safely: Who, having received such a charge, thrust them into the inner prison, and made their feet fast in the stocks. And at midnight Paul and Silas prayed, and sang praises unto God: and the prisoners heard them.

[1] Lydia Saad and Zach Hrynowski, "How Many Americans Believe in God?" 24 June 2022 https://news.gallup.com/poll/268205/americans-believe-god.aspx

And suddenly there was a great earthquake, so that the foundations of the prison were shaken: and immediately all the doors were opened, and every one's bands were loosed. And the keeper of the prison awaking out of his sleep, and seeing the prison doors open, he drew out his sword, and would have killed himself, supposing that the prisoners had been fled. But Paul cried with a loud voice, saying, Do thyself no harm: for we are all here. (Acts 16:22–28)

Here we find Paul and Silas at odds with the rulers of the Greek city Philippi over their teachings and Paul having cast a demon out of a woman causing her masters a loss of financial gain. The wording of the scriptures in Acts 16:19 is specific in that that her masters recognize that their *hope* for gain was lost. So immediately we see a loss of hope.

Because of these actions, Paul and Silas were set upon by the multitude and were beaten and thrown into jail. We see the great distress caused by loss of hope that was experienced by these rulers as they were upset enough to tear off their clothes in commanding Paul and Silas to be beaten.

They then charged the jailer to keep them "safely", meaning they were not finished with them yet and wanted to make sure they would not be able to continue in their work. The jailer took this charge quite seriously and puts them into the innermost part of the jail and securely placed their feet in stocks.

However, Paul and Silas were clearly not without hope. They were praying and singing praises to God. And not silently either. The other prisoners in the jail heard them. Paul and Silas were bold in their hope and were not afraid to let the world know it. And their hope was answered with a great earthquake that shook the very foundation of the prison and caused all the prison doors to be opened and all the shackles to open, freeing the prisoners.

The jailer, thinking that all the prisoners were secure in the prison, was asleep at the time. But being awakened by the earthquake, he arose to find all the prison doors open and the shackles unlocked.

It is at this point the jailer had no hope. He gave up and drew his sword and was about to take his own life. He saw no hope in his situation. He believed that, despite the fact that the earthquake was clearly out of his control, and even though the prisoners were all freed through no action of his own, he would still be held accountable. And because of this belief, he had no hope and saw that the only way out was to end his life.

In the midst of this scene, we have a plea of hope, and it came from an unlikely source. Paul cries out with a loud voice, "Do thyself no harm: for we are all here." Paul was saying, "Wait! There is hope!" And this hope was that "we are all here." The jailer had hope because he had not lost all the prisoners as he at first feared.

This plea for hope by Paul ensured that the jailer did not take his own life and allowed him to live in order to make another plea of his own. And because of this, it is a great plea.

The fifth greatest plea ever made: the plea to do thyself no harm, for there is hope.

THE PLEA FOR LIFE

L ife is a precious gift. Unfortunately, we have cheapened life by showing little regard for it. Wars, murders, abortion, natural disasters, famine, and disease have all combined to desensitize us to just how precious life really is.

Wars take place in the world, and we go about our daily lives despite the suffering and loss of life. We watch story after story on the evening news of horrific murders around our country and around the world. We hotly debate one another on whether a woman (a word we no longer seem to be able to define) has a so-called *right* to rip a little baby from her womb resulting in its death. We see loss of life on a large scale during hurricanes, earthquakes, floods, and other natural disasters. And famines, pandemics, and diseases such as cancer and heart disease take hundreds of thousands of lives every year.

We learn of lives lost around the world every single day. But how many of us would give up our own lives so that others may live? And how many of us would not plead for our own lives if we were faced with imminent death?

Well, we would find ourselves in good company because the creator of all life, Jesus Christ, asked God the Father if there were any possible way for Him to be spared. We will look at two passages, one from the book of John, and the other from the book of Matthew, to fully understand this plea.

> Then said Jesus unto them again, Verily, verily, I say unto you, I am the door of the sheep. All that ever came before me are thieves and robbers: but the sheep did not hear them. I am the door: by me if any man enter in, he shall be saved, and shall go in and out, and find pasture.

The thief cometh not, but for to steal, and to kill, and to destroy: I am come that they might have life, and that they might have it more abundantly. I am the good shepherd: the good shepherd giveth his life for the sheep. (John 10:7–11)

Then saith he unto them, My soul is exceeding sorrowful, even unto death: tarry ye here, and watch with me. And he went a little farther, and fell on his face, and prayed, saying, O my Father, if it be possible, let this cup pass from me: nevertheless not as I will, but as thou wilt. And he cometh unto the disciples, and findeth them asleep, and saith unto Peter, What, could ye not watch with me one hour? Watch and pray, that ye enter not into temptation: the spirit indeed is willing, but the flesh is weak. He went away again the second time, and prayed, saying, O my Father, if this cup may not pass away from me, except I drink it, thy will be done. And he came and found them asleep again: for their eyes were heavy And he left them, and went away again, and prayed the third time, saying the same words. (Matthew 26:38–44)

In the passage from John we find Jesus fully explaining His deity and His role. He likened himself to a door (in this case we might think of it as a gate) to a safe haven for the sheep. And he said that He was the only way into the safe haven of the green pastures. If any man enters in through Jesus, then he will be saved from the thieves and robbers that come to steal, kill, and destroy.

And Jesus clearly said here that His purpose in coming was that the sheep (any man who enters into the pasture through Him) might have life. And He clarified the point by saying that the life He was speaking of is abundant life, that eternal life found in the kingdom of God. And then Jesus said how that abundant life was to be obtained. Jesus was the good shepherd, and the good shepherd will give His own life for the sheep.

Here, the creator of all life, told His creation that He would give up His own life in order that the creation may have abundant life. Jesus talked of His own death on several occasions and even the specific manner of His death. Clearly the reality of the cross was no surprise to Him. He expected it. It was inevitable. And Jesus said that it was necessary so that the sheep may have abundant life and so that they might see the kingdom of God.

So why did He pray for relief in the garden? Note that in the passage from Matthew, Jesus, knew the time was at hand for Him to give up His life. He went with the disciples to the place called Gethsemane. And there he became exceedingly sorrowful, "even unto death." Jesus knew He was going to be put to death soon. And that caused Him to be sorrowful. Even the creator and sustainer of all life, when faced with His own death, which He had known about and talked about and was His purpose for being on Earth, was sorrowful at the prospect of His punishment. And knowing this, he asked His disciples to watch with Him.

Jesus separated Himself from His disciples and He fell on His face and began to plead with God the Father. Jesus became more personal with God the Father than perhaps anywhere else we read in scripture. I am sure the disciples could detect the sincerity in His voice as he pleaded "O my Father." What a moment in history. What a moment in all of time. God pleaded with himself for His own life.

Three times Jesus prayed this prayer. Three times He asked that "this cup pass from me." And three times He ended with "thy will be done." Three times God the Son fell on His face before God the Father and earnestly, passionately, and sincerely pleaded to not have to go to the cross.

This should be a powerful statement to all of creation of just how precious, how unique in all the universe, how important life really is. If the very creator of life, the very sustainer of life, and the one who gave up His own life for us would plead with the Father in heaven for His life in this manner, how much more should we be attentive to the pleas for life around us?

The plea for life is such an important one that I want to emphasize the point here for a couple of paragraphs. We need to understand that Jesus Christ gave up His own life so that *all* may have the opportunity to see the kingdom of God. Jesus said, "I am come that they might have life", that means you and me and everyone who has lived, everyone who will live—those you know, those you do not know, those you love, and those you hate. Jesus Christ died for *everyone* so that we may have life. And He gave up His own life for you and me because **all lives matter**. There is not a single life that ever has been or ever will be that is not important to Jesus Christ. And I know this because there is not a single life that ever has been or ever will be that did not come from the breath of Jesus Christ. He is the creator of all things and the sustainer of all things. And by Him all things are created and for His glory they exist.

And if God, in His infinite wisdom and glory and power, saw fit to devise a plan that required His own Son to lay down His life for those He created, then there is no other conclusion possible, but that life is a precious gift from Him and that we are all equally important to Him.

And if we—you and I and everyone around us—are that important to God, shouldn't we be equally important to each other? We grieve God the Father when we try to make ourselves more important than those around us, especially when we become the arbiters of life as in the case of abortion.

Most of us have seen the struggles of life, a seed planted in the ground that pushes out of the soil and spreads leaves that reach for the sunlight, or a hatchling bird that pecks away at its shell and breaks free and comes forth to find its mother, or a newborn puppy or kitten, that with eyes still shut, cries out and desperately crawls around seeking its mother. Life wants to survive, to carry on, and to propagate. What would make any of us think that the exact same thing is not true in the womb of the human mother? Why would we not believe that the life inside of the mother's womb is just anxiously awaiting the moment it may see its mother? One of the biggest travesties in America today is that we afford more protections to bald eagles (under The Bald and Golden Eagle Protection Act [16 U.S.C. 668-668d], enacted in 1940) than we do human babies in the mother's womb. And if you honestly believe that a bald eagle egg is more precious than a baby in the womb, then your belief perfectly illustrates how we have come to cheapen life.

But I have a question for you to consider: Do you really think that Jesus Christ, who is the creator and sustainer of all life, was so concerned with losing His physical life that He knew He would regain in three days' time, that He would plead with the Father in heaven to have that cup pass from Him?

I do not think so. It was not the physical death that bothered the Son of God; it was the spiritual death that bothered him. For the first time ever,

God the Son was going to be separated from God the Father and God the Holy Spirit. He was going to be apart from himself.

When Jesus was first put up on the cross, His thoughts were immediately to us and to those who had crucified Him. Look at his words: "Father, forgive them; for they know not what they do." He did not ask about His own needs or plight; He was thinking about you and me. However, later, before giving up the ghost, he cried out with a loud voice "My God, my God, why hast thou forsaken me?" This was the point His attention turned away from us and towards Himself, it was the point of separation from the Father. So, we see that the plea for life is more about our spiritual lives more than it is about our physical lives.

The sixth greatest plea ever made: the plea for life, the most precious gift ever given.

THE PLEA FOR SALVATION

Remember the jailer who lost all hope when it appeared that all his prisoners may have escaped when the integrity of the prison was compromised during an earthquake? We saw that his lost hope led him to almost take his own life before he was offered a plea of hope from Paul who exclaimed that all the prisoners were still there. Well, the jailer's story did not end there.

When we recognize there is hope in life, and we recognize that our lives are precious and have meaning, and we then recall that Jesus told Nicodemus that those who did not believe were already condemned, we might begin to understand that perhaps we are in peril and need to be saved.

Salvation, or the plea to be saved, seems to be one of the more sensitive subjects in all the Bible, and it really need not be. Even though, over the years, it has been preached many different ways, put into tracts, depicted in movies, and shared one-on-one on the streets, people still seem to want to make it much more complicated than it really is. But before we discuss the finer points of salvation, let's take a look at the plea.

You may recall that we last saw our jailer friend offered a plea for hope, having been charged to keep Paul and Silas "safely" in the jail. However, an earthquake caused all the prison doors to be opened and all the chains on the prisoners to fall off. These events caused the jailer to give up all hope and he was about to take his own life when Paul cried out for him to stop. And the jailer's hope was renewed when he learned that all the prisoners were still there.

This is where we pick up the story:

> Then he called for a light, and sprang in, and came trembling, and fell down before Paul and Silas, And brought them out, and said, Sirs, what must I do to be saved? And they said, Believe on the Lord Jesus Christ, and thou shalt be saved, and thy house. And they spake unto him the word of the Lord, and to all that were in his house. And he took them the same hour of the night, and washed their stripes; and was baptized, he and all his, straightway. (Acts 16:29–33)

Having just been prevented from taking his own life and given newfound hope at learning none of the prisoners had escaped, and probably with sword still in hand, the very next thing the jailer did was to call for a light, run into the jail and fall at the feet of Paul and Silas.

Stories of jailers whose lives were saved by the very prisoners they were guarding are rare. Stories of jailers whose lives were saved by the prisoners they were guarding who then run and fall at the feet of those same prisoners, are rarer still. And if there is more than one of these stories out there, this one is by far the most important. It is the most important story of a jailer having his life saved by the prisoners because it is the one story in which the jailer realized he needed to be saved.

The jailer brought Paul and Silas out of the prison and asked them a very important question: "Sirs, what must I do to be saved?" And the answer was "Believe on the Lord Jesus Christ, and thou shalt be saved, and thy house." But notice that is not the end of the story:

> And they spake unto him the word of the Lord, and to all that were in his house. And he took them the same hour of the night, and washed their stripes; and was baptized, he and all his, straightway. (Acts 16:32–33)

The jailer, being from Philippi, probably had not heard about the life of Jesus. And he probably did not know Jewish scriptures, so he probably had no context for understanding the prophesies and the coming of the Messiah. He would not have known that the God of all creation had come into the world and walked among the people. He needed to be told "the word of the Lord." Paul and Silas needed to teach him and his house the Gospel story. And then, he and his house were baptized.

Some people might argue that the plea to be saved is the greatest plea ever to be made. And they may have a point. But let me ask you a question: When someone cries out for help, what were the circumstances that caused you to require help? The radio call "MAYDAY! MAYDAY! MAYDAY" is recognized almost globally as an alert that someone is experiencing life-threatening distress. But isn't it true that the response to the call is very different if it is coming from an airplane than it is if it is coming from a ship on the ocean?

When it comes to the plea of salvation, understanding what brought us to this point, and what our condition is, becomes critical to understanding the response. In other words, in order to make use of the help provided, we need to know a little bit about ourselves and about the answer we give.

And note that the answer given, "believe on the Lord Jesus Christ" is not any different than the answer to the plea to see the kingdom of God, or the plea for mercy, or the plea for help in unbelief, or any of the other pleas. It is the one requirement that God places on us so He can determine which side of eternity we end up on. So, it makes sense to understand exactly what is being required here. And it will also explain why it was necessary for Paul and Silas to speak "the word of the Lord" to the jailer, and all that were in his house.

Let's look at Roman's chapter 10; it will help us to understand more fully the words "believe on the Lord Jesus Christ."

> Brethren, my heart's desire and prayer to God for Israel is, that they might be saved. For I bear them record that they have a zeal of God, but not according to knowledge. For they being ignorant of God's righteousness, and going about to establish their own righteousness, have not submitted themselves unto the righteousness of God. For Christ is the end of the law for righteousness to every one that believeth. For Moses describeth the righteousness which is of the law, That the man which doeth those things shall live by them. But the righteousness which is of faith speaketh on this wise, Say not in thine heart,

Who shall ascend into heaven? (that is, to bring Christ down from above:) Or, Who shall descend into the deep? (that is, to bring up Christ again from the dead.) But what saith it? The word is nigh thee, even in thy mouth, and in thy heart: that is, the word of faith, which we preach; That if thou shalt confess with thy mouth the Lord Jesus, and shalt believe in thine heart that God hath raised him from the dead, thou shalt be saved. For with the heart man believeth unto righteousness; and with the mouth confession is made unto salvation. For the scripture saith, Whosoever believeth on him shall not be ashamed. For there is no difference between the Jew and the Greek: for the same Lord over all is rich unto all that call upon him. For whosoever shall call upon the name of the Lord shall be saved. How then shall they call on him in whom they have not believed? and how shall they believe in him of whom they have not heard? and how shall they hear without a preacher? And how shall they preach, except they be sent? as it is written, How beautiful are the feet of them that preach the gospel of peace, and bring glad tidings of good things! But they have not all obeyed the gospel. For Esaias saith, Lord, who hath believed our report? So then faith cometh by hearing, and hearing by the word of God. But I say, Have they not heard? Yes verily, their sound went into all the earth, and their words unto the ends of the world. But I say, Did not Israel know? First Moses saith, I will provoke you to jealousy by them that are no people, and by a foolish nation I will anger you. But Esaias is very bold, and saith, I was found of them that sought me not; I was made manifest unto them that asked not after me. But to Israel he saith, All day long I have stretched forth my hands unto a disobedient and gainsaying people. (Romans 10:1–21)

This is the entire tenth chapter of Paul's letter to the Romans. The entire chapter explains salvation in great detail. And given that we have a plea for salvation here, it should follow that we should understand the detail. Let's look at each piece.

Paul began by expressing his heart's desire and prayer to God for the nation of Israel (verse 1). And what was that desire and prayer? "That they might be saved." Paul desired the same plea from the nation of Israel that the jailer in Philippi just expressed. And why would Paul want to hear this plea from the nation of Israel? Because they were his kinsman, his people, and because he knew they were God's chosen people to bring God's salvation into the world.

Paul saw a problem here. He said of Israel, "For I bear them record that they have a zeal of God, but not according to knowledge." (verse 2). He said that he knew the people of Israel had a desire to serve God ("a zeal of God") but not according to the correct knowledge. Think of it like this: Let's say you love the game of American football and you are knowledgeable about the rules of the game. While you are watching a game between your favorite team and their biggest rival, suddenly the referee calls a penalty against your team. And that penalty just hits you out of the blue. You had no idea there was such a rule. At that moment, you have a great zeal for American football. You love the game. But the referee, whose job it is to know all the rules by heart and to officiate the game, approaches the game with knowledge you do not possess. That was what Paul is saying here. The Israelites had a great zeal for God, but they are missing some knowledge.

Paul then explained that missing piece of knowledge (verse 3) when he told them they were ignorant of God's righteousness. God's righteousness is faith in Jesus Christ. Paul had explained this earlier in his letter in chapter 3 (Romans 3:21–22). And being ignorant of God's righteousness, the nation of Israel established their own righteousness. In doing so they did not submit to the righteousness of God.

This is an extremely important point as the exact same thing is happening in America today, and indeed, the rest of the world. People in this world are ignorant of God's righteousness; we make up our own instead. Abortion; transgender identities; LBGTQIA rights; Diversity Equality Inclusion (DEI); putting self-first and others last—these are all are part of our self-made "righteousness," but these do not reflect God's righteousness. It is important that we understand that the exact same flaw

Paul saw in the people of the world some two thousand years ago, is seen in the world today.

We should pay close attention to the next thing Paul said. In verse 4 he explained that Jesus Christ was the "end of the law for righteousness." Paul meant that the law no longer defined our righteousness. Jesus Christ now is our righteousness. But only to those "that believe."

Many people say that Christians just want to tell people how to live. And I get that some churches may seem legalistic and preach nothing but rules to follow. But what Paul was saying here in Romans chapter 10 is that, if you believe on the Lord Jesus Christ, He becomes your righteousness, and you are no longer bound to keeping the law in order to gain righteousness. However, Paul was not saying Jesus Christ "is the end of the law." He was not saying that Jesus Christ ended the law, only that he replaced the righteousness of keeping the law with Himself. And if you believe in Jesus Christ, He will work within you to then keep the law. So, Christians are not telling people how to live, rather, they are only saying that, if people believe in Jesus Christ, they will then want to live according to His doctrine. Because He will change their lives.

In verses 5–8 Paul explained that Moses brought the law from God as the standard of righteousness. And he explained that we must keep all the law—the law in its entirety—in order to achieve that righteousness. Paul then explained that the righteousness of the law may be replaced by the righteousness of Jesus Christ through faith in Him. Remember when Jesus told Nicodemus that God sent his Son into the world not to condemn the world but to save the world?

> For God sent not his Son into the world to condemn the world; but that the world through him might be saved. He that believeth on him is not condemned: but he that believeth not is condemned already, because he hath not believed in the name of the only begotten Son of God. (John 3:17–18)

Jesus was telling Nicodemus the same thing that Paul was telling the Romans here. Jesus was telling Nicodemus that not putting his faith in Jesus Christ meant he was already condemned. And Paul was telling the

Romans that, under the law, people were not found to be righteous unless they kept the entire law.

Who in all human history has never once told a lie? Any lie? Most people think that, because they have never murdered anyone, they are good and righteous. But lies, lust, not keeping the Sabbath day holy—all these things are in violation of God's law. And seeing that it is God's heaven, because He created it, He gets to define the rules whereby people (his creation) are allowed to enter it. And He defined ten simple rules: the Mosaic law. or the law Moses brought down from the mountain top to the people of Israel. And no one in all human history has ever kept all the law; neither will anyone because we all have sinful natures and are prone to sin.

In Romans 10:9-13 Paul explained how to obtain the righteousness of Jesus Christ to replace the righteousness lost by not keeping God's law.

> That if thou shalt confess with thy mouth the Lord Jesus, and shalt believe in thine heart that God hath raised him from the dead, thou shalt be saved. For with the heart man believeth unto righteousness; and with the mouth confession is made unto salvation. For the scripture saith, Whosoever believeth on him shall not be ashamed. For there is no difference between the Jew and the Greek: for the same Lord over all is rich unto all that call upon him. For whosoever shall call upon the name of the Lord shall be saved. (Romans 10:9-13)

Paul laid out faith as simply as possible. Confess, with your mouth. Confession is a verbal expression, and it involves multiple parties. Paul was not saying here that you have some obligation to seek out every person in the world and tell them about Jesus Christ (although some try and to interpret this passage that way). Neither was Paul suggesting that a mute person may not be saved. Paul was saying that belief in the heart will result in a plea from the believer. Consider what Paul said in Romans 10:13: "For whosoever shall call upon the name of the Lord shall be saved." This is a spiritual cry made in the spirit with a spiritual voice.

There is a fictional story told about a person on a trip for their place of employment. At their destination they check into a hotel and settle into their room for the night. Before turning out the light for the evening, they find a Gideons Bible laying on the nightstand with a note recommending John chapter 3. So, this business traveler picks up the Bible and finds the book of John and begins to read chapter 3. And as they read, like Nicodemus, they begin to understand their desire to see the kingdom of heaven. And as their conviction grows, they understand the truth of the Gospel of Christ and they believe in their heart. And their belief results in a cry to the Lord Jesus Christ that they may be remembered in His kingdom. There is no one around to hear them or to witness this event. They are in the hotel room alone and no one else on earth knows what they are doing at that moment. As this business traveler drifts off to sleep, they are content in the knowledge that their newfound faith, belief in Jesus Christ raised from the dead by God, and their cry to the Lord was heard. But this business traveler never left that hotel room alive. During the night a fire breaks out in the hotel and thick, toxic smoke fills the building resulting in the death of the business traveler.

The question that becomes obvious with this story is: Did the business traveler see the kingdom of heaven? And the equally obvious answer must be: Of course, he did! God is just and merciful and kind. And God would never tease us with the promise of seeing the kingdom of God and then suddenly remove the prize from us because of a technicality outside of our control. To begin with, the victory is His, not ours. And for God to introduce a condition for salvation that we could not meet, would be God robbing Himself, not us.

The answer is we are spiritually dead in our sin (see Ephesians 2:1) and belief in our hearts that God raised His Son, Jesus Christ, from the dead brings about spiritual life. And a new life, like a newborn baby, cries out for all around to hear. In this case our newborn spirit, now brought to life through faith, cries out to our spiritual father.

Belief in our heart is faith without seeing or experiencing. You may believe something because you experience it. You may know you like ice cream because you have tasted it, tried different flavors and brands, and have experienced the sensations of eating it. Because of your experience you believe ice cream is a delicious dessert. You may believe in historical figures, such as the 16th President of the United States, Abraham Lincoln. You may have seen photographs or paintings of President Lincoln and you may have read historical records of his life. But you never met President Lincoln or experienced him personally. You believe he lived and was president based off reason and the historical record. However, faith accepts a belief with no basis in experience and no physical evidence within the historical record. Your reason may tell you that there is no way you can verify that Jesus Christ was a person who lived in Israel around two thousand years ago. Your reason may tell you that there is no way to confirm His claim to be the Son of God. Your reason may tell you that you have no proof that He died on a cross between two thieves. And your reason may tell you that a person returning to life after being dead and buried for three days is a medical impossibility. But you believe it despite what is reasonable. You just know it to be true in your heart. That is faith, and that is believing in your heart. This is the type of belief that Paul talked about and said was necessary in order to see the kingdom of God.

Finally, in these verses, Paul makes it clear here that salvation is available to all. He says that God is the God of all, whether Jew or Greek.

In the next few verses Paul explained that there are those called of God to preach and to teach and to evangelize. And those individuals are held to a higher accountability. And this is the point in Romans 10 that explains the relevance of the jailer in Acts 16.

In Romans 10:14–17 we arrive at the point of understanding Acts 16:32: "And they spake unto him the word of the Lord, and to all that were in his house." In Romans 10:14–17 Paul explained why it was necessary for the jailer to hear the word of the Lord.

Paul asked a series of simple questions, "How then shall they call on him in whom they have not believed? How shall they believe in him of whom they have not heard? How shall they hear without a preacher? How shall they preach, except they be sent?"

And I would ask the same questions today. How can you believe in Jesus Christ if you have not heard the word of the Lord? Paul summed up his argument for the preaching of the gospel of Jesus Christ in one succinct statement, "So then faith cometh by hearing, and hearing by the word of God" (Romans 10:17). It is vital that people hear the word of God. Because, without that, there can be no faith.

And this becomes a revelation to us that faith is a journey, and the first step is believing in our hearts that Jesus Christ is Lord and that God raised him from the dead so that he could be the righteousness for our sins.

When you take the this step of faith and confess with your mouth that Jesus Christ is the Lord of your life and believe in your heart that God raised Him from the dead, you are beginning a journey of getting to know Him more and more in your life, every day. That is *hearing* the word of God.

In Romans 10:18–21 Paul concluded his argument for salvation with a sharp warning. Paul wrote that he has a question of his own, "But I say, Have they not heard?" And he answered this question with, "Yes, of course they have." Paul was warning us that rejecting the Gospel of Jesus Christ cannot be forgiven with the excuse of having not heard. If you have ever had the opportunity to hear the Gospel of Jesus Christ, and have rejected that opportunity, you cannot claim that you did not hear and somehow deserve additional consideration.

Chapter 10 of the book of Romans contains an awful lot to unpack. And, hopefully, I've scratched the surface of it for you. It is the focal point of all the Greatest Pleas Ever Made. And I'd like to provide you with a summary:

- **Salvation begins** with belief in a God. You become a theist in your worldview at this point. Evolution, atheism, or any other non-theistic viewpoints cannot possibly fit into your worldview because they deny a theistic worldview.
- **Salvation relies** on knowing who the right God is: The God of Abraham, Isaac, and Jacob. And God's chosen people—the Jewish nation of Israel—was used by Him to bring His Son, Jesus Christ, into the world through the linage of King David. Other gods—Buddha, Allah, the gods of Hinduism—cannot possibly fit into your worldview because they supplant Jehovah God as the one true God.
- **Salvation understands** that you are separated from that God because you have sinned against Him and that the penalty for that sin is death. Spiritual death. Eternal separation from God.
- **Salvation realizes** that "God so loved the world, that He gave His only begotten Son" (John 3:16) to pay the penalty for your

sin, and that He did so upon the cross and rose from the dead on the third day, and that, if you place your faith in Him, you will have everlasting life.

- **Salvation starts** with a faith resulting out of a belief in your heart that God raised His Son, Jesus Christ, from the dead; that He became your righteousness; that He paid the price for your sins; and that He is the Way, the Truth, and the Life; for you to see the kingdom of God.

- **Salvation continues** with confessing Jesus Christ as Lord—Jesus Christ who thought it not robbery to be equal with God. Jesus Christ who stated that He and the Father in Heaven were one. When you confess Jesus Christ as Lord, you are recognizing Him as God in the flesh come to earth. You cry out to the Lord in your spirit to see the kingdom of God.

- **Salvation becomes** a journey in your life: To hear the word of God, to know the word of God, and to know more and more about Jesus Christ in your own life. The journey becomes one of knowing an infinite God. And in the kingdom of God, you will have an eternity of study.

Salvation comes about when you recognize that you are not just some cosmic accident that happened to pop into existence. It begins with an understanding that you are created by God and that the vastness of the universe is a display of His majesty and glory. Salvation comes by discovering that God is the God of Israel and the God of the Holy Bible. Salvation comes when you recognize that you have sinned against God. And salvation comes when you understand His great plan to provide eternal life to you through His Son, Jesus Christ.

And salvation comes when you recognize the need for salvation in your own life. When a people arrive at the point at which they understand that they cannot possibly see the kingdom of God without Jesus Christ, that is the point they cry out, "What must I do to be saved?"

The seventh greatest plea ever made: the plea to be saved.

THE PLEA TO NOT BE HINDERED

No one likes to be restrained. We all want to be free to move about as we see fit. Who of us; who drive cars can say we are thrilled to be pulled over by a police officer in a traffic stop? Most of us are just as annoyed at having our journey hindered as we are that we are probably going to have to pay a fine.

People do not like to be hindered in their journeys, and there is no exception for those who follow the Christian life. For people who have experienced the salvation of Jesus Christ, there is a desire to move forward, to know and understand what comes next, to not be hindered but to jump right in and take the next step of the journey.

And we find such a story of a person who did not want to be hindered in his journey. It occurred two thousand years ago and is recorded in the book of Acts. It is where we find our next great plea:

> And the angel of the Lord spake unto Philip, saying, Arise, and go toward the south unto the way that goeth down from Jerusalem unto Gaza, which is desert. And he arose and went: and, behold, a man of Ethiopia, an eunuch of great authority under Candace queen of the Ethiopians, who had the charge of all her treasure, and had come to Jerusalem for to worship, Was returning, and sitting in his chariot read Esaias the prophet. Then the Spirit said unto Philip, Go near, and join thyself to this chariot. And Philip ran thither to him, and heard him read the prophet Esaias, and said, Understandest thou what thou readest? And he said, How can I, except some man should guide me? And he desired Philip that he would come up and sit

with him. The place of the scripture which he read was this, He was led as a sheep to the slaughter; and like a lamb dumb before his shearer, so opened he not his mouth: In his humiliation his judgment was taken away: and who shall declare his generation? for his life is taken from the earth. And the eunuch answered Philip, and said, I pray thee, of whom speaketh the prophet this? of himself, or of some other man? Then Philip opened his mouth, and began at the same scripture, and preached unto him Jesus. And as they went on their way, they came unto a certain water: and the eunuch said, See, here is water; what doth hinder me to be baptized? And Philip said, If thou believest with all thine heart, thou mayest. And he answered and said, I believe that Jesus Christ is the Son of God. And he commanded the chariot to stand still: and they went down both into the water, both Philip and the eunuch; and he baptized him. ³And when they were come up out of the water, the Spirit of the Lord caught away Philip, that the eunuch saw him no more: and he went on his way rejoicing. (Acts 8:26–39)

At the beginning of this story, Philip was confronted by an angel of the Lord telling him to go down from Jerusalem to Gaza, into the desert. Sometimes God sends us into the desert without explanation. And it is up to us to follow God's path in order to discover His plan. And this is exactly what Philip did. He did what the angel of the Lord told him to do, and he met a man of Ethiopia but not just a citizen of Ethiopia. This man was a eunuch of great authority under Candace, the queen of all Ethiopians. And this man had charge of all the queen's treasure. So, we discover that God intended for Philip to meet a man of great influence in Ethiopia, which Philip accomplished by obeying the angel of the Lord. This, I think, is a great point in the story because sometimes, in order to not be hindered in our own lives, it is important that we not hinder God in His great plan.

We learn that the man from Ethiopia had come to Jerusalem to worship. He was seeking the kingdom of God, just as Nicodemus had. And his curiosity had led him to Israel and to the City of David, Jerusalem. It is interesting to me that, at this point he found a copy of the book of Isaiah. If you consider the fact that scrolls of the day had to be painstakingly copied by hand, and that those copies were considered sacred, for a man from Ethiopia, even a very influential man, to gain a copy of a sacred scroll must have been divine providence indeed.

But he did have a copy. And he was not content with waiting until he arrived back home to open it and read it. Instead, he was reading it in his chariot on the ride home. And Philip, being instructed to draw near to the chariot, heard him reading aloud. Someone who reads a book aloud is intent on paying attention to every word. And so we know that the man from Ethiopia was paying close attention to what he read.

Philip seized upon this opportunity to enter a conversation with him by asking him if he understood what he read. This affirms the truth that Paul stated in Romans chapter ten that people could not believe if they had not heard, and how could they hear without a preacher? People in the world today may spend a lot of time reading the word of God with little to no understanding at all, but without someone appointed by God to illuminate the word to them, they cannot hear. The story of the plea for salvation bears this out. Paul explained that some have been appointed as pastors and teachers. The man from Ethiopia needed a preacher, and God sent Philip to help him understand the word of God.

And we know that the Ethiopian needed clarification because of his answer. He looked at Philip and asked how he could understand the writing without someone to explain it to him. And seeing that Philip was knowledgeable of the scriptures, he invited him to join him in the chariot.

Just as the jailer needed Paul and Silas to preach the word of God to him, so the Ethiopian needed Philip to preach the word of God. This is why our churches, our missionaries, and our evangelists are so important. Without people to preach the word of God, a lost and dying world would have no hope.

The book of Isaiah was written more than seven hundred years before Philip found the Ethiopian reading it in his chariot somewhere south of Jerusalem. Recall that each copy had to be made by hand. To give us an idea of how many copies there may have been in Jerusalem at the time of the Ethiopians visit, there were twenty-one copies found in the Qumran caves between 1947 and 1956. If we assume a population of two hundred (to use round numbers), there would have been about one copy of the book of Isaiah for every ten people. The population of Jerusalem at the time of the Ethiopian's visit may have been around thirty thousand (although there are widely varying estimates from multiple sources). If we assume the same ratio (several of the Qumran copies were most likely produced at Qumran and not brought with them to the site, meaning the Qumran ratio may be high) we could assume there were about three thousand copies of the book of Isaiah at the time of the Ethiopian's visit. Three thousand copies of a book in a city of tens of thousands is not a lot. Could the inhabitants of Jerusalem have spared one copy for a dignitary from Ethiopia? Sure, they could. But it most likely came at a price, the Jewish priests would not have been very eager to give up even one of their copies without some kind of gain. And yet, by the divine appointment of God, the Ethiopian obtained a copy, which he was taking with him as he traveled back home, and he was reading from this passage found in Isaiah chapter 53 at the time Philip joined him.

> All we like sheep have gone astray; we have turned every one to his own way; and the Lord hath laid on him the iniquity of us all. He was oppressed, and he was afflicted, yet he opened not his mouth: he is brought as a lamb to the slaughter, and as a sheep before her shearers is dumb, so he openeth not his mouth. He was taken from prison and from judgment: and who shall declare his generation? for he was cut off out of the land of the living: for the transgression of my people was he stricken. (Isaiah 53:6–8)

And the Ethiopian could not have known—would not have known—what this passage referenced. Indeed, the religious leaders in Jerusalem who had Jesus crucified, failed to understand the significance of this passage as it played out before their very eyes. Here is how it is recorded in the book of Acts:

> The place of the scripture which he read was this, He was led as a sheep to the slaughter; and like a lamb

dumb before his shearer, so opened he not his mouth: In his humiliation his judgment was taken away: and who shall declare his generation? for his life is taken from the earth. And the eunuch answered Philip, and said, I pray thee, of whom speaketh the prophet this? of himself, or of some other man? Then Philip opened his mouth, and began at the same scripture, and preached unto him Jesus. (Acts 8:32–35)

So, the Ethiopian asked Philip to explain it to him. And just as Jesus explained to Nicodemus, and the certain man with the demon-possessed son, and Paul and Silas explained to the jailer, Philip began to expound upon the Holy Scriptures. And we are told he "preached unto him Jesus." Note that this is from the Old Testament which was written prior to the book of Acts being written. And Philip concluded that the Holy Scriptures were pointing to Jesus.

As Philip concluded his explanation of the Holy Scriptures, they come upon a body of water. And here is where we find the plea of the Ethiopian—the plea to not be hindered:

And as they went on their way, they came unto a certain water: and the eunuch said, See, here is water; what doth hinder me to be baptized? And Philip said, If thou believest with all thine heart, thou mayest. And he answered and said, I believe that Jesus Christ is the Son of God. And he commanded the chariot to stand still: and they went down both into the water, both Philip and the eunuch; and he baptized him. And when they were come up out of the water, the Spirit of the Lord caught away Philip, that the eunuch saw him no more: and he went on his way rejoicing. (Acts 8:36–39)

When the Ethiopian heard Jesus Christ preached; and the prophecy of Isaiah, he immediately wanted to be baptized. They came upon a body of water, and the Ethiopian asked Philip, "so what is hindering me to be baptized?" He wanted to know what obstacles were in his way. He wanted to know if there was anything he had missed that had not been accomplished yet. More importantly, he wanted to move on to the next step.

When we are hindered in life, it is important that we understand what the hindrance is and how we must deal with it. And as the Ethiopian asked Philip, we might just go to God and ask Him what hinders us in our lives. If we do not ask, we may never learn how to deal with the roadblocks in our lives; we might end up living in frustration. When we understand what we believe, the next step in our lives should be to go to God in prayer, and ask, "Here is the water, Lord. What is hindering me?" I believe God will answer that prayer and show you how to get to the next step.

And we see that the Ethiopian received his answer from Philip, and just as we have now seen with plea, after plea after plea, the answer to the plea not to be hindered is "If thou believest with all thine heart." Note that the Ethiopian was not ashamed to confess with his mouth as he immediately answered Philip saying, "I believe that Jesus Christ is the Son of God."

The Ethiopian was baptized by Philip. The Spirit of the Lord takes Philip away as they were coming up out of the water; the Ethiopian never saw him again, and he went on his way rejoicing.

Many times, obstacles and hindrances keep us from rejoicing in our journeys. We become frustrated with being hindered in our journey. We want to move ahead but cannot. And if we were to just ask God to show us what hinders us and how to deal with it, then we can confess Jesus Christ Lord, get on with the next step in our journey, and go on our way rejoicing. We need to be mindful of when God brings a Philip into our lives, if only for a season, to help us with our understanding.

The eighth greatest plea ever made: the plea to not be hindered in our journey.

THE PLEA FOR TRUTH

We all want to know the truth. Truth is important to our decision making and how we live our lives. And the absence of truth can be devastating. In order for us to make sound decisions and effect good outcomes, we must know as much of the truth as possible. Truth can have a lasting effect on our lives for years or even decades to come. There is one critical point at which our very lives hang in the balance and depends on knowing the absolute truth. And that critical point is where our own mortality meets all of eternity. Job said it like this:

> O that thou wouldest hide me in the grave, that thou wouldest keep me secret, until thy wrath be past, that thou wouldest appoint me a set time, and remember me! If a man die, shall he live again? all the days of my appointed time will I wait, till my change come. Thou shalt call, and I will answer thee: thou wilt have a desire to the work of thine hands. (Job 14:13–15)

The question all people contemplate at some point in their lives; If I die, will I live again? Job said he would wait all the days of his appointed time until that transformation came from death unto new life.

But truth can be hard to come by. Facts change, and our understanding changes with them. We cannot even get the truth about our climate and weather. Some predict great calamities in the world due to global climate change while others are skeptical of the facts presented. Even facts that we have supposedly solidified for all time, like the earth is round, are questioned by some who present opposing points of view that the earth is flat.

And then there are truths that we alter to align to our own sense of reality. The Holy Scriptures tell us that people are created either male or female. But there are some who would have us believe that we can change genders if we do not like what others have identified us as. We are told that, if a person is born a male, and chooses to be a female, then that becomes the new truth. Even though no one has yet to show that people can change their DNA: females have an XX pairing of chromosomes and males having an XY pairing. This leaves one to wonder what *truth* will take precedence in a court of law when a defendant who was born a biological male, but has chosen to live as a female for most of his/her life is involved in a trial in which DNA evidence points to a male having committed a crime.

But the biggest challenge to all truth is lies. The Bible addresses this like no other belief system in all human history, telling us that it is Satan who is the father of all lies. The very first lie in all recorded human history was told by Satan to Eve. God had told Adam and Eve a certain truth: Eat of the tree of Knowledge of Good and Evil and you will surely die. But Satan came along and told Eve that God had lied and that neither she nor Adam would die if they ate of the fruit. Eve was confronted with two conflicting stories. On the one hand God had said that, if they ate of the fruit, they would die, and on the other hand Satan had said that, if they ate of the fruit they would not die. One statement was the truth, the other statement was a lie. Eve decided to gamble on the lie. She then brought Adam into the destructive behavior by giving him the forbidden fruit to eat. Adam ate the fruit of the tree of Knowledge of Good and Evil, and sin entered the world. All because of a lie. Adam and Eve did not adhere to the truth.

And the Bible tells us that Adam was not beguiled (or deceived) as Eve was deceived. In other words, Adam knew the truth and chose to disobey God despite the consequences. So, knowing the truth is not enough. It is what we do with truth and how we act upon it that is important.

Since that moment in the Garden of Eden; when Eve chose to gamble on Satan's lie and Adam chose to go along with Eve despite knowing God's truth, lies have been a part of all human existence. Someone once said, "Show me one person in all of human history who claims to have never told a single lie within their lifetime, and I will show you a liar." People say that you cannot lump all people for all time into a single category.

And yet I will tell you that every single person who has ever lived, who is alive today, and who ever will live, has lied (or will lie) at some point in his or her lifetime. And it is because of these lies that we require a court system in order to meter out justice. For the most part, courts distinguish between truth and lies.

Such was the case some two thousand years ago when Jesus Christ found himself standing in Pilate's court. And it brings us to our next great plea, the plea for truth. It is found in John chapter 18:

> Then led they Jesus from Caiaphas unto the hall of judgment: and it was early; and they themselves went not into the judgment hall, lest they should be defiled; but that they might eat the passover. Pilate then went out unto them, and said, What accusation bring ye against this man? They answered and said unto him, If he were not a malefactor, we would not have delivered him up unto thee. Then said Pilate unto them, Take ye him, and judge him according to your law. The Jews therefore said unto him, It is not lawful for us to put any man to death: That the saying of Jesus might be fulfilled, which he spake, signifying what death he should die. Then Pilate entered into the judgment hall again, and called Jesus, and said unto him, Art thou the King of the Jews? Jesus answered him, Sayest thou this thing of thyself, or did others tell it thee of me? Pilate answered, Am I a Jew? Thine own nation and the chief priests have delivered thee unto me: what hast thou done? Jesus answered, My kingdom is not of this world: if my kingdom were of this world, then would my servants fight, that I should not be delivered to the Jews: but now is my kingdom not from hence. Pilate therefore said unto him, Art thou a king then? Jesus answered, Thou sayest that I am a king. To this end was I born, and for this cause came I into the world, that I should bear witness unto the truth. Every one that is of the truth heareth my voice. Pilate saith unto him, What is truth? And when he had said this, he went out again unto

the Jews, and saith unto them, I find in him no fault at all. But ye have a custom, that I should release unto you one at the passover: will ye therefore that I release unto you the King of the Jews? Then cried they all again, saying, Not this man, but Barabbas. Now Barabbas was a robber. (John 18:28–40)

We will pick up the story with Jesus being brought from Caiaphas, the high priest, to the hall of judgment, what we would call a courthouse or courtroom today. There is no doubt that Jesus was on trial there. He was being forcibly brought to the courthouse for no other reason than to be put on trial. And we know right from the beginning that the fix is in. The trial was but a mockery as the accusers had already made up their minds and delivered a guilty verdict. Notice that they led Jesus to the hall of judgment however, "they themselves did not go into the judgment hall because they did not want to be defiled before the Passover." I'm not quite sure we can all see the irony of their actions in claiming that entering into the judgment hall would defile them before eating the Passover dinner; yet, they were perfectly fine with their lies about the charges of crimes Jesus was supposed to have committed. Being the religious rulers of the day, they had to have known the commandment "Thou shalt not bear false witness." (Exodus 20:16). But somehow violating this commandment did not quite raise to the level of defilement as entering the judgment hall would have.

In almost every single court in the world today, we recognize the right of the accused to be faced by their accusers. This right was not afforded to Jesus in this trial. Instead, Pilate, the judge in this case, was forced to exit the courtroom to ask the accusers what the charges were. The judge in the case did not even know the charges he was about to adjudicate. And note the answer he was given, "They answered and said unto him, "If he were not a malefactor, we would not have delivered him up unto thee." (John 18:30). The accusers could not even state the charges against the accused to Pilate. Instead, they gave a platitude claiming, in essence, "Hey, if he were not guilty, he would not be here." This again reaffirms that they had already reached a guilty verdict before the trial began.

Pilate must have seen though this self-serving answer because he immediately told them to try Jesus by Jewish law since they could not specify the charges that Jesus was guilty of under Roman law. But once again the religious leaders betrayed themselves; their answer to Pilate was that they could not do that because it was unlawful for them to put any man to death. They were bold enough to not only tell Pilate that Jesus was guilty before the trial began simply because they said so and had brought Jesus to him, but also what manner of punishment they demanded for their false charges.

Pilate then went back into the courtroom and began the very solemn task of determining the truth in a trial. He began with the one charge he must have heard from the religious leaders, asking Jesus if He was indeed *"King of the Jews?"* Jesus, knowing that he was not facing his accusers in the court of law, and knowing that no matter how He answered, it would simply be His word against the word of the religious leaders, asked a question of his own. He wanted to know in what context Pilate was asking the question. Jesus wanted to know if Pilate was asking the question of his own accord, or if it was because others had told him that he should ask the question.

Pilate delivered a platitude of his own at that point. He answered Jesus's question by asking Him if he was a Jew. And then he told Him that His own people had brought Him to the court. And in a kind of desperation to get at the truth, he told Jesus that His own nation, even the chief priests, had brought Him to the court, so He must have done something wrong. Obviously, Jesus was guilty or else He would not be there. Pilate was beginning to buy into the lie told by the chief priests. But he was still lacking a charge, so He asked Jesus "What have you done?" Think about that for a moment and then try to recall any other court case in which the judge asks the accused to please tell the court what crime he or she has committed.

And Jesus obliged Pilate with an answer. Jesus, did indeed say that He had a kingdom, which would imply that He was a king: however, it was not the kingdom for which He had been accused of claiming. Jesus told Pilate that His kingdom was not of this world. And to prove that point, He basically said to Pilate, "Look, if my kingdom were here, of this world, then would not my servants fight so that I would not be delivered up to the Jews?" Jesus was pointing out to Pilate the whole fallacy of the charge made against Him. If He were indeed a king, then He would have a king's army to protect Him and keep Him safe.

Pilate obviously understood this argument, realizing that a true king would have loyal subjects and would not be standing in a courtroom alone. Unfortunately, Pilate became hung up and fixated on the first two words: *my kingdom.* Jesus had clearly said that He had a kingdom, even if it was not the one related to the charges, He was facing. Pilot said to Jesus, "So you are a king then?" This was most likely a rhetorical question. Pilate realized that if Jesus said He has a kingdom, then He must be a king.

But Jesus answers in a peculiar way. Jesus looked at Pilate and said, "Well, have not you yourself said that I am a king?" I can almost imagine Jesus standing there, looking at Pilate, and thinking, *Isn't that what all of this is about? You and the chief priests saying that I am a king?* Jesus had just told Pilate that His kingdom was not of this world. He did not say that He was the king of the Jews. And Pilate had seized on that and said, "Ah-ha! So, you are a king?" And Jesus said, "You say so."

The trial should have been over at this point, but Jesus decided to add some clarification to the argument for Pilate to consider. Jesus volunteered some information and told Pilate, "To this end was I born, and for this cause came I into the world, that I should bear witness unto the truth. Every one that is of the truth heareth my voice" (John 18:37). Jesus said, in essence, "Look, Pilate, I'll tell you exactly why I am here. From my birth I have been in this world to bear witness to the truth. And those that know the truth will know that I am speaking it." Pilate, probably exacerbated by not getting to the truth in this trial, made a great plea. What is truth? Pilate just wanted to get to the truth.

But Pilate did not wait for an answer to his plea. Instead, he had found another way out. He went out and told the chief priests, "Look, I find no fault in this man." This, essentially, was a verdict of not guilty. But he had a way of putting the onus back on the chief priests; he invoked a Passover custom that allowed for any one prisoner to be released. And he gave the priests a choice between a thief and Jesus. They, of course, chose the thief and demand that Jesus be crucified. How frustrated Pilate must have been that he never did get to the truth.

We should never miss the fact that Jesus Christ came into the world to testify unto the truth. And what truth is that? The same truth that He told Nicodemus: in order to see the kingdom of God, you must start with belief in the Son of God.

Of all the truths in the world, this is the most reliable, the most important, and the one that will never change. We can argue all the cases we want to, in all the courtrooms of the world, and there will never be a greater truth discovered than the fact that Jesus Christ is the Son of God and died to be our righteousness in place of the law.

Obviously, He was tried unjustly if even the judge found that He had committed no crime. And if Jesus Christ could go through that on our behalf, should not we at least consider His own words: "I am the Way, the Truth, and the Life. No one comes to the Father except through me" (John 1:6)?

Isn't it worth getting to the truth? Jesus is the one truth in your life that will seal your fate for all of eternity. And we all should solidify it in our lives today. I have a favorite saying when someone dies. I'm not sure that it is all that original to myself, but I do know that I find myself using it way more than anyone else around me. I usually use it when a well-known personality like Carl Sagan or Dr. Stephen Hawking dies. Someone who was adamantly atheist in his or her worldview and denied God, especially Jesus Christ. When their deaths are announced, I am prone to say, "Well, (*fill-in-the-name*) now knows the truth." And I say this with all sincerity and soberness. It works for anyone, and yes, when Dr. Stephen Hawking's death hit the news, I said, "Well, Dr. Stephen Hawking now knows the truth." Because it is the one truth that is answered for you when your life is over.

Do you want to be like Eve in the garden and gamble on a lie from Satan, or do you want to pursue the truth?

The ninth greatest plea ever made: the plea for truth.

THE PLEA TO KNOW GOD

Who doesn't want to know God? There are those who embrace an agnostic world view who probably just don't care. Even atheists will challenge the theists to show them God if they can. There was an interview with a world-renowned evolutionist; who was an unwavering atheist. His argument was, how could he not be an atheist given his great faith in evolution? He would state that evolution leaves no room whatsoever for a God. During the interview, he was asked what he would say to God were he to die and find out he was wrong and was now standing before God. His answer: "I would ask him why he stayed so well hidden."

Everyone would like to know God; the desire is built into our beings. But, as with all things, the trials and the successes are in the details. There are multiple claims about who (or what) is God. There are challenges as to whether there even is a God. And of course, there is the question of Satan or the devil. If God has an adversary, does that adversary have a role in us knowing God? I wouldn't even want to hazard a guess as to how many books we would have to write just cover the basics on the path to knowing God. It's a rather complicated task. But then God is a complicated being.

There is one thing I know for sure, though, and that is that God is not well hidden. As a matter of fact, He's not even standing in the shadows, or in the clouds, or behind the mountains, or under the sea. He is not hidden at all. He is right there in plain sight for all to see. If you look to the shadows, His light will illuminate all darkness. If you look to the clouds, you will see His covenant and promise. If you look to the mountains, you will see His majesty and glory. And if you look under the sea, you will see His mystery and wonder. God is all around, for those who look and truly want to see.

People who do not search for God have no hope. Leading researchers like Dr. Stephen Hawking and Dr. Richard Dawkins have adamantly made the case for there being no God. However, if you follow the case for there being no God all the way out to its end logical conclusion, then you must ask yourself why they even care. If there is no God, no higher being, no intelligent design, then everything is meaningless. There are some very smart people in the world and they will argue for both sides: evidence of a created world or evidence of an evolved world. They argue the physics, the biology, and the geology. And they go back and forth with point and counterpoint "proving" their theories are correct.

I wish they would put all of that aside and realize just one small thing; without a God, we are left with nothing but the observable forces in the universe—just what we can see, smell, taste, hear, touch, and reason with some level of understanding. And if that is true, then everything is simply the byproduct of matter bumping into other matter and causing some type of reaction, that should be explainable by physical and quantum laws within the universe.

Dr. Stephen Hawking has passed away and now knows the truth. Dr. Richard Dawkins, however, should consider that, at some point, an atom bumped into another atom (for whatever reason, whether it be the big bang or some other event we haven't thought up yet), and those atoms began to form molecules, and those molecules began to form different forms of matter, solids, liquids, and gasses. And all of that came together to eventually form plants, animals, and humans. And eventually, one day those atoms bumping into each other managed to produce Dr. Richard Dawkins, completely at random (following natural laws of course), but without design, without meaning, and without purpose. It is just a natural event, nothing more and nothing less.

And if that is true, then where is the meaning? Even the fact that people try to prove or disprove one theory or another has absolutely zero meaning. It is all just one big cosmic event. There is no intelligence, all those thoughts that Dr. Richard Dawkins has about disproving God; were all predetermined eons ago when one atom just happened to bump into another atom in a certain way that eventually led to several atoms coming together to form some random human that seems to have "thought."

It is just so ironic to me that people who believe they are the by-product of some random, natural, cosmic event, with absolutely no meaning or purpose behind their existence, spend so much time—or any time at all—trying to disprove the existence of a god. Why would they do that? Why does it matter? And why would one even care? It is all meaningless, right?

We can either live in the meaningless world of Dr. Richard Dawkins, or we can live in the world of hope provided by a god, a creator, a higher being than ourselves or what we witness around us. Because that world has a purpose—the purpose provided by the Creator Himself. And for the theist, arguing the existence of God does have meaning, especially when it comes to understanding the purpose of the creation.

And thus, people have a plea to know God. Why am I here? What does it all mean? Is there a heaven? Is there a hell? Will I live for all of eternity? Is there something more beyond just this physical life? These are all pleas to know God. Our very beings cry out to know God and know what our relationship with Him is. We want to have hope, purpose, and meaning. And that is answered only through a God; there is no other way.

And of all the religions that lay claim to revealing the one true God, only Christianity acknowledges and answers that plea to know God. And I do not believe this is by accident. I believe God—Jehovah God—protects His claim on being the one true God. And no one else, no other being, can infringe upon that claim no matter how hard they try. And it would only follow that the one true God would want to show purpose and meaning to his creation.

So, there is no wonder, then, in our plea to know God. It is the natural yearning built into us by the creator Himself. And this plea came from Philip directly to Jesus Christ:

> If ye had known me, ye should have known my Father also: and from henceforth ye know him, and have seen him. Philip saith unto him, Lord, show us the Father, and it sufficeth us. Jesus saith unto him, Have I been so long time with you, and yet hast thou not known me, Philip? he that hath seen me hath seen the Father; and how sayest thou then, Show us the Father? (John 14:7–9)

Jesus was speaking to the disciples and he told them rather bluntly,

"If you had known me." I love it when people tell me, "You do not know me." It presupposes that they believe I am trying to get to know them in the first place. It also makes an indirect assumption that I am either making a judgment or drawing a conclusion about them that they do not believe is somehow fair for whatever reason. And their defense to these pure perceptions, which they have no way of validating, is to lash out with "You do not know me." What they do not know is that God the Father knows them better than they know themselves. And I know God the Father.

But how would you like to have God in the flesh, the very Son of God, look you straight in the eye and say, "You do not know me"? Jesus told His disciples, "You do not know me, because if you did know me, you would also know my Father. And by knowing me, you know the Father and have seen him."

Philip was still reaching a little bit rather than understanding what Jesus had just told him, and tells Jesus that, if He would just show them God the Father, their plea will be answered, they would be satisfied, and all would be well with the world. Even after Jesus had just told him, "If you know me, you know the Father."

And Jesus probably just shook His head as he looked at Philip and once again said, "Philip, you do not know me." Jesus even pointed out the long time they had spent together. He said it had been a "long time," meaning "We have been together long enough for you to know me by now." And so, Jesus told Philip, "He that hath seen me hath seen the Father." In other words, "Look, Philip, you've already seen the Father. You're looking at Him right now." And there must have been disappointment in His voice as He asked, "How can you say, Show us the Father?"

Jesus, still speaking to His disciples of the Father, continued to make the point that to know Him is to know God the Father.

> These things have I spoken unto you in proverbs: but the time cometh, when I shall no more speak unto you in proverbs, but I shall shew you plainly of the Father. At that day ye shall ask in my name: and I say not unto you, that I will pray the Father for you: For the Father himself loveth you, because ye have loved me, and have believed that I came out from God. I came forth from the Father,

and am come into the world: again, I leave the world, and go to the Father. His disciples said unto him, Lo, now speakest thou plainly, and speakest no proverb. Now are we sure that thou knowest all things, and needest not that any man should ask thee: by this we believe that thou camest forth from God. Jesus answered them, Do ye now believe? (John 16:25–31)

Jesus told His disciples that, in the past, He had spoken to them in proverbs and parables, but that the time would come when He would speak to them plainly of the Father. Jesus told them that when they asked something in His name, they were asking in the Father's name. He told them, that He would not ask the Father on their behalf, because the Father already loved them just as they love Him and believe that He came from God. And He told them, I came from God, and I will go back to God, and I'll come into the world again. He was telling them plainly of His death and resurrection.

And suddenly His disciples wanted to seem enlightened. And I'll just bet that it was Philip that looks at Jesus and says, "Well finally, you stopped speaking in proverbs and started giving it to us straight." And because of this one statement by Jesus, the disciples could state with certainty that they were sure Jesus knew all things, and that no man could ask a question He could not answer, and because of that, they now believed He came from the Father in heaven.

I wonder what the inflection in Jesus's voice was when he looked at them and said, "Do ye now believe?" It was only two chapters earlier that Jesus had looked at Philip and said, "You do not know me." Not too much time had passed since that statement, and we wonder how much more intimately the disciples now knew Jesus than they did just a few minutes or hours earlier.

We must remember that, when we say, "You do not know me" we are being harsh and judgmental. And we are presupposing facts about the other people we have no way of validating ourselves. When we say, "You do not know me" we rarely stop to think that if we do not believe others have had enough time to "know us," then we certainly haven't had enough time to "know them." When we say, "You do not know me" we are, in fact, making an equal and just as sharp a judgement about ourselves.

But this is not the case with Jesus Christ. When Jesus looked at Philip and essentially said, "You don't know me" He was saying it from the position of the Creator. He was saying it from the standpoint of purpose and meaning, knowing that, rather than the atoms that made up the molecules, that made up the cells, that made up Philip being random and some cosmic accident, that it was He, Jesus Christ, who had not only put every single one of them in place, but sustained them all even as they stood there and talked.

When Jesus said, "You do not know me" He said it with a compassion that means, "Why do you not know me? I want you to know me in the same way I know you. Do you not know I created you to have a relationship with you and to have you to know Me?"

God created us. He shaped that vacuum inside of us for a reason. It is so that we would want to know Him. We would seek Him out. We would plead, "Oh Lord I want to know God! Please show me God the Father!" And we can do that with believing on Jesus Christ. We can also do that by exploring God's creation around us. God's infinite creation shows us the infinite creativity of an infinite Creator. And an infinite eternity seems just about the right amount of time to get to know an infinite God.

The tenth greatest plea ever made: the plea to know God.

THE PLEA FOR PEACE

P eople of the world generally want to live in peace. The problem is we believe we cannot have peace unless it is "our" peace. Think about every major conflict in the history of the world. Both sides want peace. But they do not believe they can have peace unless it is on their terms.

Wars and conflicts are demonstrations of mankind not believing they can have peace unless competing ideals and practices are eliminated. For some, peace cannot be achieved unless they are in control and have vanquished all that they cannot live in peace with.

This is a direct revelation of the spiritual battles that exist in our lives. The battles stem directly from godliness and ungodliness as embodied in the beings of God and Satan. There is a mistaken belief that Satan can provide us peace and that belief in Jesus Christ cannot. But Holy Scripture tells us otherwise.

All conflict is a result of rule—who will rule our lives and who will be in control. Take the abortion conflict for example. Those who find some sort of "right" in women ripping a God-created child from their wombs, are worshipping at the altar of child sacrifice of Satan himself. Satan hates all of God's creation because he knows that God created humankind to have a relationship with Him. And this is cause for great jealousy in Satan's heart because he cannot create. He cannot have his own creation to have a special relationship with him and so he results to stealing God's creation. And in doing so, he lies and persuades us to believe that a child in the womb is somehow not God's creation and it is therefore acceptable to sacrifice the child to him on his alter. It is Satan worship at its deepest roots.

Christians, on the other hand, acknowledge the rule of God in their lives. And recognizing God as sovereign and the creator of all life, they hold life as precious and sacred, a gift of the creator Himself. And in doing so, they want to uphold God's commandments and not murder innocent and precious lives.

And so, we end up with conflict.

And while no one takes any joy in conflict, it does reaffirm biblical truth to me. No other dissertation on human existence more accurately describes the human condition and the world than does Holy Scripture.

The atheistic worldview certainly has no explanation of or solution for conflict at all. And yet even godless atheists want peace. One would wonder why since there is no purpose or meaning to existence in their worldview. Isn't it odd that atheists argue that God and Satan are made up in fantasy and fable yet use them to try to explain the conflict we see in the world?

If atheists were to seriously consider that argument, they should realize that they are ascribing way more intelligence to humans who existed more than four thousand years ago than they themselves exhibit today. After all, to come up with a force for good and a force for evil and have it propagated all around the world and last for all of human history to date, is quite a feat.

Meanwhile all the "enlightened" people today try everything under the sun to explain conflict in the world. And they believe they can come up with cures for it, which is in direct violation of their worldview to begin with. When atheists try to come up with a "cure" for anything they deem wrong with the human condition, they have no choice but to believe that they themselves are acting on predetermined random acts ordered by a natural world. Independent of a god, they can have no other rational explanation.

Where evolutionists will argue for the appearance of intelligent design in the world, I can just as credibly argue for created intelligence in the world. What evolutionists believe is that intelligence is just the result of random atoms bumping into each other in the natural world, independent of a Creator. Under this worldview nothing that we experience in life would make any sense, including, and especially, conflict.

But while atheists have no hope for the future or for peace, Christians do have a plea for peace in their lives and may achieve peace in the midst of conflict. And that peace does not come from us, but rather from God Himself; He brings peace into our lives so that He may maintain a good relationship with us. When we place our trust and faith in Jesus Christ, we enter a relationship with the Creator of the universe who is at peace with His creation because He is in control, and everything is according to His plan. And that relationship brings His peace into our lives.

> Behold, the hour cometh, yea, is now come, that ye shall be scattered, every man to his own, and shall leave me alone: and yet I am not alone, because the Father is with me. These things I have spoken unto you, that in me ye might have peace. In the world ye shall have tribulation: but be of good cheer; I have overcome the world. (John 16:32–33)

Here we find Jesus still talking with His disciples. He was about to tell them why He was speaking so plainly to them, as we last saw. He was about to go to the garden of Gethsemane to pray. And from there He will be taken, and eventually crucified. And so He wanted to warn His disciples that things were going to be bad. There is about to be conflict.

And not just conflict, but conflict that would scatter them to the wind; He would be left alone. We find out that everything He had been telling them was to comfort them so that they might be at peace.

The very first thing we see here is that the disciples did not ask for peace even though they should have. They had things on their mind: "Show us the Father. Speak plainly to us and not in proverbs." They were oblivious to the conflict that was about to happen. So, we do not see the disciples making a verbal plea for peace. But we do see that Jesus knew they needed it. And perhaps Jesus was thinking to himself, "If you knew what was coming, you would be asking for peace." And Jesus told them that His purpose for telling them all these things is so that they would be at peace.

Oftentimes we do not know when conflict is going to arise in our lives because it can be hard to see the storms on the horizon. But we know there are going to be storms. It is so much harder to ask for peace after the war has already started. We see this in major conflicts all the time. A war breaks out and people all over the world immediately start calling for peace talks. Perhaps if we had seen the war coming, we could have held the peace talks before it even started.

And other times when we are sure there is going to be a war, we still fail to enter into peace talks before the actual conflict. There is just something about humans that does not seem to allow them to think of peace until after a war has already started. But Jesus knew the disciples were about to experience great conflict; He knew that their situation was going to become very bad very quickly, so, He prepares them beforehand so that they might be at peace.

The second thing we see here is that Jesus set expectations by telling the disciples what was going to happen. There is nothing more likely to destroy the peace in our lives than disruptions and surprises, so, Jesus took the surprise away by giving the disciples a spoiler alert. Information can be powerful. And knowing something is about to happen, whether we can change it or not, can go a long way toward helping us prepare for whatever bad thing is going to happen.

So many times, we act surprised when disaster strikes when, really, we shouldn't. Jesus told His disciples, "In the world ye shall have tribulation" and I do not believe this was any special message directed at just the disciples and no one else. Jesus was saying "you" as in "you and me today"; we will have tribulation in this world. People want to think, *It doesn't mean me*, but Jesus said "you". And it is hard to separate "you" from "yourself".

We will all experience tribulation in this world. We may not find ourselves crucified upside down like Peter, or shipwrecked like Paul, or thrown into the lion's den like Daniel, or on a battlefield somewhere caught in a war. But we will find ourselves in tribulation. Whether it is being cut off in traffic, having an argument with a best friend, or a disagreement with a family member.

And knowing this, why wouldn't we plead for peace before the conflict even comes? Jesus Christ wants to bring peace into our lives. He plainly tells His disciples, "These things I have spoken unto you, that in me ye might have peace." And He told them this *before* the conflict began. And he wants you and me to have peace in our lives as well.

The third and final point we see in this passage is that we can be of good cheer. Our peace is not a sad, depressed peace. Our peace is a cheerful, happy peace. Jesus tells his disciples to be of "good cheer."

In the world, we are usually content to live in peace begrudgingly. Individuals on both sides of any given conflict crawl off to their respective corners and mope. We sulk, we brood, we drown in our own self-pity, but rarely are we cheerful to just live in peace. When are we cheerful? Usually in victory. When our team wins, when our country wins the war, we are wildly cheerful, and we celebrate.

And here Jesus tells His disciples to be of good cheer in their peace. Why? Because He has overcome the world. He has won the battle. And God is in control. So be at peace.

The eleventh greatest plea ever made: the plea for peace.

THE PLEA FOR JOY

Of course, with peace comes the opportunity for joy. And God wants us to be joyful because He himself is joyful. And our joy, our happiness, does not have to stem from the things of this world that are temporal. We have a hope that extends beyond this world; it is rooted in the eternalness of God.

Joy is a problem for the non-believer. I would ask atheists where their joy comes from, but every answer given would be based on the physical aspect of life and not the spiritual. Since atheists do not believe in God, their joy is only brought about by what exists within the physical world and how it interacts based upon physical laws.

And because of that, we have a world that has lost more joy today than probably at any other point in history. Consider the joyless people in the world all around us and the reasons they have no joy. Take those who are consumed by Global Climate Change alarmists. There are young adults in the world today who have completely lost all hope of joy because they would rather trust in a lie of Satan rather than the truth of Jesus Christ.

And these people have really lost all joy. Groups of them have taken to all kinds of destructive measures in protests such as pouring out gallons of milk in grocery stores and throwing cans of soup on historic works of art. Where is the joy in any of that? There really is none. And if they really are sincere, then we are led to believe that they are acting out in this way because they believe they have no future. And why is that? Because they have no hope in Jesus Christ, and without hope there can be no joy.

The whole Global Climate Change debate is another perfect example of the spiritual warfare the world experiences all the time. Here is how: Satan tells us lies in order to get us to turn away from the Lord and these lies cause us to lose our joy. Lies like evolution and Global Climate Change are designed to get us to abandon all hope in the Lord Jesus Christ.

Evolution does this by trying to get us to believe that the creation story is a lie. So, these godless people tell a lie that claims the truth of God is a lie. And we get caught up in this spider's web of lies. And once evolution has asserted itself as the rightful explanation for the universe, it conveniently points out to us that it accomplished this without a god. And then says we are delusional and have been brainwashed by religion.

Of course, it does this without producing a single thread of evidence. "Scientists" break their own rules and claim their theories as fact when indeed they are impossible to prove. Oh sure, they can weave a pretty good tale and point to a whole bunch of observations, but at the end of the day, that doesn't make any of their theories true or factual.

Does any of this sound familiar? It should because it is the exact same argument that they themselves use to deny the existence of God. And we buy into their hypocritical arguments. And they do this without explaining to us why they even care. It doesn't mean anything after all. If there is no god, then everything we experience is just the randomness of the natural universe and it means nothing at all. There is no hope. And that includes *joy* as well. Joy is meaningless in this world. It is just a physical and chemical reaction. Nothing more, nothing less.

The Global Climate Change debate gets us to abandon all hope in God through fear. The world is going to end; there is going to be fear and pestilence throughout the world. The oceans are going to rise and wipe out entire cities and eventually entire populations. And we must act now—right now—to fix it and stop all of this from happening. And if you are not on board with this theory, you are a Global Climate Change Denier and need to be silenced.

Except that the Global Climate Change champions have been wrong time and time and time again in all their predictions. From Paul R. Ehrlich (author of *The Population Bomb*, 1968) to Paul F. Watson (founder of the Sea Shepherd Conservation Society), to former United States vice president Al A. Gore (author of *An Inconvenient Truth: The Planetary Emergency of Global Warming and What We Can Do About It*) we have heard prediction after prediction of the demise of planet Earth. The Breitbart News website published an article by John Nolte chronicling the list of failed predictions over decades.[2] In this piece John Nolte claims that climate disaster predictions have been wrong fifty-three times for more than fifty years now. Perhaps if the Global Climate Change champions had a more accurate record behind them, there wouldn't be so many Global Climate Change deniers.

The latest prediction of doom and gloom for the Earth due to Global Climate Change gives us just twelve years, and we're already two years in. We can liken predictions like this to a scenario involving a fully loaded semi-trailer truck traveling at one hundred miles per hour down an interstate highway. If someone suddenly yelled "Stop!" when the truck was just 120 feet away from a traffic jam that has caused vehicles to block the highway, the truck, of course, would not be able to stop. It could not stop. It would not stop. No matter the amount of braking the driver applied, how hard he turned the wheel, or even if the tractor trailer jackknifed and the truck turned over. At that speed and weight, it would inevitably slam into the stopped traffic in front of it. But this is exactly the picture the alarmists paint. Is it any wonder then that young minds panic and are gripped in fear?

We can easily see the results of the cries of doom and gloom for over fifty years now as young people the world over feel entitled to act out against society all in the name of Global Climate Change. Satan's lie has caused us to take our eyes off Jesus Christ and place our trust in the world. And this has resulted in us losing our hope and joy.

However, where Satan brings lies and fear, Jesus brings hope and joy. And in the same manner He told His disciples that He wanted them to have peace in their lives, He also told them He wanted them to have joy.

> These things have I spoken unto you, that my joy might remain in you, and that your joy might be full. This is my commandment, That ye love one another, as I have loved you. Greater love hath no man than this, that a man lay down his life for his friends. (John 15:11–13)

---

[2] John Nolte, "Climate 'Experts' Are 0-41 with Their Doomsday Predictions *UPDATE 0-53*" September 09, 2019 https://www.breitbart.com/environment/2019/09/20/nolte-climate-experts-are-0-41-with-their-doomsday-predictions/

Note that Jesus told His disciples that He is telling them these things that *His* joy might remain in them. For those in Christ Jesus, joy is not dependent upon the circumstances within the world. The rest of the world may panic over the lies of Satan, but Christians have hope because God is in control, and He gives us His joy.

Jesus has already told us we would go through tribulations in this world. But that is okay because, at the same time, He has told us that He has overcome the world. This means that everything is proceeding according to His plan. Our trust and our faith and our hope are to remain in the Lord. And for that, we have great joy.

But Jesus did not just come that His joy would remain in us, but also that our joy would be full. It is not a partial joy, or a joy that is for a season only. It is a full joy that overflows from us and spills out into the rest of the world. Christians should be showing the rest of the world the joy and hope of Jesus Christ, because His joy in us fills us to the brim and then overflows. His joy in us is complete and stands in the face of tribulation and carries us through. We know that God has promised to never again destroy the world through a great flood. But we also know that whatever God allows on this Earth is all in His plan and there is nothing humankind can do to interfere with that.

And what are we supposed to be doing while the rest of the world is without hope and has no joy? Well, Jesus told the disciples what He expected of them. He said that He had a commandment. And I'm sure we are to take the commandments of God seriously. That commandment is to love one another even as He has loved us. And Jesus emphasized this point by stating that the greatest love would be to give up our own lives so that others may live. This is exactly what He did for the world on the cross.

So, while the world is in a panic over Satan's lies, we are to love the world even as Christ loved the world. And isn't this consistent with the Gospel message? Whereas God so loved the world that He gave His only begotten Son, so now the Son tells us that He is sending us into the world to love even as He loved. And what could bring more joy into the world than the love of Jesus Christ? And how are we to carry out that commandment if we are in a panic, have no hope, or do not have the joy of Jesus in our hearts?

And when we know this, the plea for joy becomes a very important thing in our lives. Jesus tells us that He said all these things that His joy might be in us, and that joy might be full. So why wouldn't we cry out to God to fill us with His joy?

And what about Satan's lies? Well the book of Revelation tells us that one day we *will have* global climate change.

> And the second angel poured out his vial upon the sea; and it became as the blood of a dead man: and every living soul died in the sea. And the third angel poured out his vial upon the rivers and fountains of waters; and they became blood. And I heard the angel of the waters say, Thou art righteous, O Lord, which art, and wast, and shalt be, because thou hast judged thus. (Revelation 16:3–5)

Personally, I believe Satan is lying to the world today in order to set the stage, so that when God's judgement is poured out upon the world, the cry will be that we did not heed the warnings of those that believed Satan's lies and now we are suffering the consequences of our own actions.

And this is quite sad because, even in the midst of seeing Biblical prophecy unfold before our very eyes, people of the world will still deny God and cling to the lies of Satan and say, "There is no god."

However, even during tribulation or times of trouble, Christians can be filled with the joy of Jesus Christ.

The twelfth greatest plea ever made: the plea for joy.

THE PLEA FOR LOVE

We all want to be loved. And yet the world today cries out more and more for love every day. And the more we cry out for it, the less we understand it. How can we all be searching for love and yet not find it anywhere in the world? We all want more love in the world, but it seems nowhere to be found.

I have a confession to make at this point. While *The Greatest Pleas Ever Made* is my first completed book to be published, it is not the first book I ever set out to write. As a matter of fact, it is not even the second book, or the third, or even the fourth or fifth. This work is the sixth work that I believe God has laid on my heart. But, because of the times we live in, and the state of the world today, I believe the time is right and that this should be the first of my works people have an opportunity to read.

So, what is the first book I believe that God laid on my heart? I believe that work will be called, *And Then There Was Love*. And hopefully, God willing, that work will also soon make its way to bookshelves where you will have the opportunity to critique it if you so desire.

So, why am I making this confession now? It is simply to point out that the plea for love is big enough to fill an entire volume of its own. Frederick M. Lehman wrote the hymn "The Love of God" in 1917. The song expresses the impossibility for humankind to ever sit down and write of the love of God. However, these few short pages will be my attempt at a synopsis of humanity's plea to be loved.

The biggest problem we face in finding love in the world today is our definitions. We do not know what love is because we've overloaded the word love. This means we have made the word responsible for describing far more concepts and ideas than one word is capable of.

Comedian Leo Anthony Gallagher Jr, who passed away November 11,

2022 during the writing of this work, was fairly popular in the mid-1980s. He simply went by the stage name Gallagher. One of his main routines was based on the English language. He would point out funny constructs like "see (s-e-e)" as in what you do with your eyes, and then say "No. 'Sea' (s-e-a)" as in a large body of water. It was very funny stuff.

The potential confusion and frustrations that might arise over the use of see and sea are a result of the constructs of the language. The rules for spelling, pronunciation, and use dictate that both words have the same pronunciation, different spellings, and totally different meanings. The word *love* has been given a whole variety of meanings because of the way we have used the word over time.

We like to say, in very broad terms, that we "love" everything (I love ice cream!). But do we really "love" everything? Jesus used a word in describing the object of God's love that is translated as the English word world:

> For God so loved the world, that he gave his only begotten Son, that whosoever believeth in him should not perish, but have everlasting life. (John 3:16)

The word translated as "world" here is the Greek word *kosmon* (or *kosmos*) from which the English word "cosmos" derives. It literally expresses the entirety of creation—the universe that we live in, which is perfectly valid for a Creator. God can certainly express His love for all His creation. However, the Greek word *kosmon* was not translated to the English word *universe* here. It was translated as the English word *world*, which narrows down the focus from the great big cosmos around us to one specific object in the cosmos, and that object happens to be the planet we live on. But our understanding of the "object" of God's love is embodied in the word *whosoever* (which is literally the word *everyone* from the Greek) which narrows the focus down from the world itself to the inhabitants of the world; specifically, humankind, people. And yet John still recorded the word used by Jesus in the Greek as the word *kosmon*.

Let's contrast that to the way we say we "love" ice cream. In my home, ice cream is a common desert. After dinner, my wife will typically say "Would you like a bowl of ice cream?" To which my response has always been, "I *love* ice cream!". But that love is always short lived because I get only a small bowl of ice cream, and that bowl of ice cream is gone in a short amount of time. It is consumed and loses its properties to be loved.

And when I say "I love ice cream" every night, what am I really saying? That I love *all* ice cream? That would not be true as I am specific in the brands of ice cream I prefer. Am I saying that I love ice cream more than any other desert? That also would not be true as I probably would not choose the ice cream if I were given a choice between ice cream and a properly made key lime pie or coconut cream pie (although I admit the choice would be very tough). Am I saying that I would give up my life for ice cream? That would defeat the point since the ice cream would still be here even though I would not be alive to enjoy it.

So, what do I really mean when I say, "I love ice cream"? Probably that I enjoy ice cream a whole lot and that I like it as one of my regular deserts. But not that I "love" ice cream. So why is it okay for Jesus to say that God loves the *kosmon* (cosmos) and not for me to say, "I love ice cream"? I believe the answer to that is God created the cosmos. He created this great big universe (we can see only a fraction of it, and we know hardly anything about it) and He loves His creation. But He specifically sent His Son to rescue you and me, and all the rest of humanity. I, on the other hand, did not create the ice cream I like so much. I simply purchased it at the store. And while I did purchase it for my pleasure, I'm not sure I'd compare my pleasure in consuming ice cream to God's pleasure in His creation.

So that is a simple example. When we say we "love" ice cream—or cake, or sitting on the lake early in the morning, or walks in the woods during fall, or going to the football game on Friday night, or playing games with friends, or the myriad other things that we express "love" for—it is easy to understand what we are saying and what we mean.

But what about other uses? Am I obligated to "make love, not war"? This slogan or motto, which was used over and over again during the 1960s by those who didn't take the time to stop and think about what they were saying and whether or not it made any sense, is completely warped.

To begin with, the idea that "making love" is somehow accomplished through sexual activity (which is what the slang implies and would have you believe) is the worst thought-out argument of all time. If we are to accept the association of the slang use of making love then we would have to conclude that there is not enough sexual activity in the world to fill the world with love. Furthermore, aside from the slang use of the phrase, can anyone tell me how to "make love"? How is love made? And I know there are people reading this right now who are trying to formulate an answer in their minds. You should just stop. Because the answer is that, we humans cannot *make* love. We can be vessels for love. We can channel love. But we cannot create love of our own accord.

And this is because love is not all those things we associate it with. Love is the essence of God:

> Beloved, let us love one another: for love is of God; and every one that loveth is born of God, and knoweth God. He that loveth not knoweth not God; for God is love. In this was manifested the love of God toward us, because that God sent his only begotten Son into the world, that we might live through him. (I John 4:7–9)

Love is of God. And that is because God is love. And we can be filled with God's love, and God's love can flow through us into the rest of the world, but there is nothing we can do to create love in and of ourselves. If we could, then why wouldn't we fill the world with love? And if the answer to that is because not all of us want to or can, then would those of you who have the magic love potion, the ingredients to love, the recipe for love, either please whip up a batch big enough to fill the world, or share the secret with the rest of us so that we can do it? We have become so warped in our thinking that we really believe all we need is "Love Potion Number Nine" and everyone will just fall in love.

The second part of that phrase, "not war", is completely off base as well. Do you really believe we should not go to war in order to defend what we love? Should we not protect our families, our property, our country? Is that what love is? No security, no protection, living in fear? Of course, we should go to war to defend that which we love. That is why God has an army:

> And I saw the beast, and the kings of the earth, and their armies, gathered together to make war against him that sat on the horse, and against his army. (Revelation 19:19)

God's army will one day go to war. Granted, it will be the last war ever fought, but the army will protect and serve. Because that is what armies do. War is not the antithesis of love. War is an expression of protecting that which we love.

These expressions that we use pertaining to love harm our thinking and our ability to express what God wishes to express through us. And one last example of this is hate. We are led to believe that the opposite of love is hate. But this is not true. More accurately, hate is the complement of love. A complement completes something or makes it perfect.

Should I not hate all the sin in the world? Should I not hate my own sin? Do I have to love pain and sorrow? Do I have to love being around those that do not share my ideals or my beliefs? Of course not. To say that all is love without hate makes no sense. I cannot love that which I hate, and I cannot hate that which I love. The two complement each other.

We see this in politics all the time. One side or the other brands the opposing party as hateful because they do not agree with them. And then they claim the opposing party has no love. They are harmful for the county. And yet we love the country and are without hate. This ludicrous argument presupposes that both sides cannot love the country if they have opposing ideas of how to best care for it. And when people do this, they never acknowledge that they are expressing the same hateful sentiment that they are decrying.

The true opposite of love is lust. If you are filled with lust, as Satan is, you cannot love. And if you are filled with love, as God is, you cannot lust. God is love, and lusts for nothing. Satan is not love and lusts for everything. The opposite of love is embodied in the lust of Satan.

The biggest problem we have with overusing the word *love*, is that we've allowed Satan's lies about love to creep into our understanding of love. We believe the lie that we can make love and thus, no longer need Jesus for our love. We believe the lie that, if we hate we do not love. And so, we end up trying to love those things that we should not. And we believe the lie that we can express our own lustful desires and that everything is fine if we love, all the while not realizing that the lust in our hearts is chasing out the love of God.

> In this was manifested the love of God toward us, because that God sent his only begotten Son into the world, that we might live through him. Herein is love, not that we loved God, but that he loved us, and sent his Son to be the propitiation for our sins. Beloved, if God so loved us, we ought also to love one another. (I John 4:9–11)

The love of God was manifested—made real—toward us through Jesus Christ, His Son, so that we might *live* through Him. Love gives life. And where there is no life, I doubt you will find love. And we are to take God's love in us and share it with all the world. Because that is what life does. It procreates. It continues and multiplies and spreads.

The thirteenth greatest plea ever made: the plea for love.

THE PLEA FOR BREAD
AND WATER

We are beings made for replenishment. We constantly need to have essential items replaced in our lives. Recently, in March 2021, a new world record was set for the longest period of time a person has held his or her breath. The record time was twenty-four minutes thirty-seven seconds. While this is impressive, it is still less time than a person may go without sleep, which is estimated to be about eleven days. And while a person may go without sleep for eleven days, that is still less time than a person may go without food, which may range from eight to twenty-one days. Which may seem incredible, but when you think about it, we cannot survive even one month out of the year without breathing, sleeping, or eating.

And that is because we were designed to require replenishment. And while the evolutionists are going to claim that we evolved that way, I do not believe the evolutionists have looked at the entire picture. Because we not only need replenishment in the physical realm, but we also need to be replenished in the emotional realm (our souls), and the spiritual realm. And when you consider all three areas, the evolutionary theory looks to be a bit lacking, and creationism begins to make a lot more sense.

So obviously we need to constantly be renewed in our bodies in the physical realm. We've mentioned breathing, sleeping, and eating as just three examples. There are a host of things that our physical bodies require, and we must constantly work to make sure those needs are met. However, there are also things that our souls require. Our souls—essentially our minds, will, emotions—the part of us that bridges the gap between our spirit (that part of us that connects with God) and our bodies; and it is largely responsible for our moods and our feelings. And our souls are in constant need of replenishment.

How many of us has ever just hugged our spouses once—only once—and thought to ourselves, "*That's it. I'm good forever now*"? Or how many of us get up in the morning, get ready for work, and before we head out the door, tell our spouse, "Hey, we kissed at the wedding. No need to repeat that now."? How many of us go to one movie in our lifetimes and think that we've seen all the movies we ever need to see? Or ride a rollercoaster once and (assuming you enjoyed the experience) never feel the need to ride another ever again? Or if you like to paint or knit or create sculptures, are satisfied with the first project and never need to make another? We need to return to the things we enjoy, the things that motivate us, in order to replenish the excitement, the energy, the drive.

We do not watch Monday night football because it provides us physical nourishment, neither does it help us connect with God or sustain our spirit. And yet we immerse ourselves in the game and cheer on our favorite teams. Why? If you are watching on TV, the teams playing certainly cannot hear your cheers. But we still get excited and scream and shout anyway. Why do we do that? Because it replenishes our souls.

The spirits of Christians are alive and well and are replenished when we pray, when we meditate on Holy Scripture, and when we praise God. Singing praises to God is one of the most uplifting things we can participate in. It replenishes the soul; it replenishes the spirit. And the Bible tells us that God inhabits the praises of His people. Praising and worshiping God is probably the best way to replenish the soul and spirit at the same time because it is what we are designed for.

If you are not a Christian, then your spirit is dead. Jesus told Nicodemus that those who did not believe were already condemned. This is because the spirits of unbelievers are already dead in sin:

> And you hath he quickened, who were dead in trespasses and sins; Wherein in time past ye walked according to the course of this world, according to the prince of the power of the air, the spirit that now worketh in the children of disobedience: Among whom also we all had our conversation in times past in the lusts of our

flesh, fulfilling the desires of the flesh and of the mind; and were by nature the children of wrath, even as others. (Ephesians 2:1–3)

Something that is dead obviously does not need to be replenished. What a dead spirit needs is a rebirth. And this is exactly what Jesus was explaining to Nicodemus.

There is one particular replenishment, however, that is universally enjoyed. And that is a shared meal. All of us love to eat and drink. There are at least fourteen references to Jesus sharing meals. He ate with religious leaders (Luke 7:36). He ate with tax collectors (Luke 19). He ate with His disciples (Luke 22). And we will eat with Him in the kingdom of God (Luke 14). There is just something about sharing a meal that brings people together and replenishes our bodies and our souls. And this is something Jesus was keenly aware of, as we see in the story about Jesus feeding the people:

> When the people therefore saw that Jesus was not there, neither his disciples, they also took shipping, and came to Capernaum, seeking for Jesus. And when they had found him on the other side of the sea, they said unto him, Rabbi, when camest thou hither? Jesus answered them and said, Verily, verily, I say unto you, Ye seek me, not because ye saw the miracles, but because ye did eat of the loaves, and were filled. Labour not for the meat which perisheth, but for that meat which endureth unto everlasting life, which the Son of man shall give unto you: for him hath God the Father sealed. Then said they unto him, What shall we do, that we might work the works of God? Jesus answered and said unto them, This is the work of God, that ye believe on him whom he hath sent. They said therefore unto him, What sign shewest thou then, that we may see, and believe thee? what dost thou work? Our fathers did eat manna in the desert; as it is written, He gave them bread from heaven to eat. Then Jesus said unto them, Verily, verily, I say unto you, Moses gave you

not that bread from heaven; but my Father giveth you the true bread from heaven. For the bread of God is he which cometh down from heaven, and giveth life unto the world. Then said they unto him, Lord, evermore give us this bread. And Jesus said unto them, I am the bread of life: he that cometh to me shall never hunger; and he that believeth on me shall never thirst. But I said unto you, That ye also have seen me, and believe not. (John 6:24–36)

This story begins after Jesus has already departed from the people. When they discovered that Jesus was gone, and His disciples also, they immediately set out to find Him. They travel by boat to the other side of the Sea of Galilee to Capernaum, a city on the opposite shore from where they had been. And they found Jesus there and show their concern that He had left them. Note how they asked when he had traveled to the other shore.

Jesus replied with a very interesting response. He told them that He knew they did not follow Him to Capernaum because of the miracles that they had seen, but because of bread they had eaten, which had filled them up. It was because of the meal that the people followed Jesus to Capernaum. And that is the power of a meal. It stays with us. We are more prone to forget miracles that are right in front of us than we are to forget a good meal.

And then Jesus made another surprising statement. He told the people to not plead (labor) for food (meat), which is short lived (perishes), but rather for the food that endures in everlasting life. And He told them that this food that endures comes from the Son of Man (Himself) because God had sealed Him (He came from God).

And so, the people asked Him, "What do we need to do?" Just like Nicodemus, these people wanted to see the kingdom of God. And just like Nicodemus, they got the same answer: *believe*. We constantly see people searching for the kingdom of God, and the answer is always the same: *believe on Jesus Christ the Son of God.*

And we are still reacting today the way those people reacted to Jesus. We want a sign that will cause us to believe. Jesus just told them that they didn't follow Him because of the miracles they'd seen. You would like to think that comment would have jogged their memories. Didn't any of them think, *Oh yeah! There were all those miracles you performed*? And in a completely baffling statement, they told Jesus that Moses had fed their forefathers in the desert. What in the world is going on here? Didn't these people follow Jesus all the way to Capernaum because he had fed them in the desert? Didn't Jesus even acknowledge that they had followed Him because they had been fed? And the "sign" they were looking for was to be fed?

I believe the people were ignoring the message here. They had eaten one of the best meals of their entire lives and they were looking for more. They were trying to get Jesus to feed them more bread. But Jesus told them that they ought to be pleading for the bread from heaven because the bread from heaven gives life to the world.

Jesus is that bread of life. And when we plead for that bread and water, we will never be hungry and will never thirst.

The fourteenth greatest plea ever made: the plea for bread and water.

THE PLEA FOR COURAGE

Have you ever felt dejected? Defeated? Felt as if the whole world was against you? Have you ever felt as if the entire world has just gone crazy? And does any of that just seem like overwhelming odds that you must face? You get up in the morning and turn on the news and are greeted with instant depression. You then climb into your car to head off to work and are met with rampant road rage. You arrive at work and are faced with lack of earnings reports and potential downsizing. You are worried about how much longer you will have your job as you climb back into your car only to face more road rage on your way home. And of course, when you arrive home, your family looks at you and cheerfully asks, "How was your day?" You could just scream. And you are expected to get up and do it all again tomorrow.

Where does anyone find the fortitude to get through that? You could use a shot of courage—a bit of mental strength to face the difficulties of the day. Usually when we think of courage, we think of brave warriors who thrust themselves into harm's way in the heat of battle in order to save or protect their fellow service members. We tend to believe that courage is demonstrated only on the battlefield or by the firefighters who rush into burning buildings, emergency medical technicians who risk the hazards of the storm in order to save the sick and injured, or the police officers who walk into harm's way during a bank robbery in order to free and save a hostage.

These are the things we typically associate courage with. However, courage—which is defined as the mental strength to face danger, fear, or difficulty—is exhibited by more than just the uniformed service member, the firefighter, the EMT, or police officer. Courage is sometimes exhibited by all of those around us, and we are just unaware.

Christians are engaged in a spiritual battle that is described as not being of flesh and blood, but is a very real battle indeed. And since we are engaged in that battle, we might ask if we are part of an army, an air force, a navy, or other organized fighting force in that battle. And if we are, do we have battle gear? Turns out we do:

> Put on the whole armour of God, that ye may be able to stand against the wiles of the devil. For we wrestle not against flesh and blood, but against principalities, against powers, against the rulers of the darkness of this world, against spiritual wickedness in high places. Wherefore take unto you the whole armour of God, that ye may be able to withstand in the evil day, and having done all, to stand. (Ephesians 6:11–13)

Paul told the Ephesians that God had provided them armor. Armor is provided to fighting forces. If you are not in the fight, the military is reluctant to provide you armor. This is because armor is an expensive and specialized component of the fighting force and should be reserved for those that need it the most, those directly involved in the fight. And if we have armor, and we are engaged in a war, then we might also ask if we have any warriors of courage on our side. Do we need warriors with courage?

The answer is, of course we do. But the problem is that too many Christians fail to see the urgency or the reality of the war. We do not recognize the bombs exploding around us. We fail to see the arrows killing those around us on the battlefield. And when we do not recognize we are in a battle, we do not see the need to put on any armor, and we certainly do not see the need for courage.

But the battle is real, and even though it is against "principalities, against powers, against the rulers of the darkness of this world, against spiritual wickedness in high places", it is still manifest in the physical world. We should not ever think that a spiritual battle does not have consequences in the physical world. And we should never ever think that those real-world consequences do not affect us personally.

Do we need courage in these battles? Well, Peter described our adversary as a lion seeking to devour. And I don't know about you, but I believe it would take a little bit of courage for me to face a lion. And I was an expert shot in the military:

> Casting all your care upon him; for he careth for you. Be sober, be vigilant; because your adversary the devil, as a roaring lion, walketh about, seeking whom he may devour: Whom resist stedfast in the faith, knowing that the same afflictions are accomplished in your brethren that are in the world. (1 Peter 5:7–9)

Even with the confidence that your rifle can easily kill the lion at a distance, even with the confidence of your abilities to hit a target at a distance time and time again, and even with the knowledge that the lion is out roaming around and looking to devour you, lion hunting is not an easy task. And Peter cautioned us to remain sober and vigilant.

So, what are some of these spiritual battles that we see manifest in the real world? And how do they play out? I have already mentioned a few earlier in this work, so we can do a quick review to find examples.

Evolution is a spiritual battle. Why is evolution a spiritual battle? Is it not directly contrary to Holy Scripture? There is absolutely no room for evolution in the Holy Bible, not even from the factions that try to force fit it into Genesis by theorizing that God simply used evolution as the mechanism of creation. Evolution is a lie generated by Satan. We want to believe that evolution is a theory that originated with humans. And that is what the adversary—the devil—wants you to believe.

No serious teacher of evolution has any room for God whatsoever. And those who try to force fit God into evolutionary theory are laughed out of the room by those who teach the science. To evolutionists, God is a delusion. And by extension, those who believe in God are not rational; they are incapable of competent thought. And yet we do not want to upset the apple cart. We cannot "argue with the science" after all. And so, we try and co-exist in the enemy's camp. All because we are without armor and without courage.

And Satan's lie of evolution is carried forward by the fools who deny God, and this weakens our faith and our belief. We begin to question or alter the truth that God created the world in six twenty-four-hour days, each day measured by the Earth spinning three hundred sixty degrees on its axis one time. And we even end up arguing among our spiritual brethren as to what Genesis, in fact, really says. That's a spiritual battle. On the one hand we have the truth of God, and on the other we have the lies of Satan.

The impact in the real world of this spiritual battle is enormous. It drives a wedge between our schools and our churches, our educational systems and our religious institutions. It plants doubts in the minds of our children, and it makes it difficult to train up children in the way they should go. It is a dangerous battle that is born in the spiritual world and that plays out in a very real way in the physical world.

Abortion is a spiritual battle. Abortion is directly opposed to the idea that it is God who creates life in the womb. And that is a lie from Satan. The abortion argument would have you believe that a woman has the "right" to kill an innocent little baby in her womb. But supporters of abortion can never tell you where this "right" comes from. They just assert that it is there. They never acknowledge that Judge Harry Blackmun wrote in the opinion for the majority that the right was found in the penumbra, literally the shadow of an eclipse. Given the logic of the court, we might wonder what other rights are lurking in the shadows of our governing documents.

Clearly our Creator would never grant a right to the creation to murder that which is made in His own image. And God has not. The sixth commandment: "Thou shalt not kill" (Exodus 20:13). This means that we should not murder or take an innocent life. This is exactly what abortion does. So, the lie from Satan—it's okay kill the baby in your womb—is diametrically opposed to the truth of God, thou shalt not kill.

And the horror of this spiritual battle is born out with very real consequences in the real world. The legalization of abortion created a decline of 4.3 percent in births in American states in which abortion had previously been illegal. We are told that a birth rate of 2.11 births per woman is necessary to sustain a population and the United States statistics are slightly below that rate. Abortion is most likely a contributing factor. A very real consequence of abortion is putting entire populations into decline.

But there are other consequences as well. Abortion encourages the destruction of the nuclear family and home. Fathers' lives are destroyed along with those of the mothers. The lives of young women are destroyed as they come to grips with the reality of having killed their babies. There are the countless lives lost that could have contributed to society. And there is the massive economic impact of abortion clinics all over the United States. These efforts fuel (fund) other efforts such as transgenderism, gay and lesbian identities, and even euthanasia. Abortions also cheapen the value of life and has led to a society that treats life frivolously and with little regard. These are real consequences of a spiritual battle in a physical world.

Global Climate Change is a spiritual battle. Global Climate Change promotes the idea that humankind is in control of the fate of the Earth and not God. It destroys faith in the Creator and destroys people's hope. This is a spiritual battle also opposed to the truth of God. No longer does God sustain His creation, but instead has given it over to those who were made in His image. And we are led to believe that we have the power to literally destroy the Earth upon which we live and to wipe out all, or most all, creation.

This spiritual battle is causing divisiveness and conflict within our societies. It is causing young people who have no understanding of either the science or theology to revolt against society and to act out in inappropriate ways. This is a very real spiritual battle with very real-world consequences.

These are just a few of the battles that are occurring in our world today that are turning the souls of men and women away from God. These are battles that are sealing the eternal fate of entire generations and are straining our churches.

And they occur because Christians have refused to put on the whole armor of God, unite as a single military with Jesus Christ as the head, and because they have refused to act with courage. Do we need to plead for courage today? I believe the evidence is clear that we do.

> And the Lord shall give them up before your face, that ye may do unto them according unto all the commandments which I have commanded you. Be strong and of a good courage, fear not, nor be afraid of them: for the Lord thy God, he it is that doth go with thee; he

will not fail thee, nor forsake thee. And Moses called unto Joshua, and said unto him in the sight of all Israel, Be strong and of a good courage: for thou must go with this people unto the land which the Lord hath sworn unto their fathers to give them; and thou shalt cause them to inherit it. (Deuteronomy 31:5–7)

If we are to inherit that which God has promised us, we must act with courage. And it is not that we stand in our own strength, but rather that God provides His strength in us. Note that Moses told the people, "And the Lord shall give them up before your face." We can have courage because we stand in the might of the Lord. And so, Moses told the people to "Be strong and of a good courage".

This courage comes from belief in the Lord Jesus Christ. We can face the fear and difficulty because we know we are on the right side of eternity. We know what God has commanded, and we know the lies of Satan. And when facing the roaming lion seeking to devour, we can stand with the courage of the Lord and confidently put on the whole armor of God knowing that He is in control.

When we plead with God for courage to face our spiritual battles every day, we are acknowledging that God knows there is a battle waging, and He is the predetermined victor.

The fifteenth greatest plea ever made: the plea for courage.

THE PLEA FOR STRENGTH

Acting with courage is important, but if you do not have the strength to act, courage is all for naught. Strength on the battlefield is important in any conflict, and our military goes to great lengths to be able to project strength around the world.

The same is true in our spiritual battles. We need strength to be able to fight and carry on. We grow weary spiritually just the same as we grow weary physically. And we need spiritual renewal just as we need physical renewal. So many Christians today are in tune with physical fitness. We know what to eat, how much to eat, when to eat, and how much exercise we need. People spend time, money, and energy on ensuring they are physically fit and in good health. But then they spend no time ensuring they are spiritually fit and in good spiritual health. And we do this individually and without regard for the body of Christ as a whole.

I saw a documentary once about the United States Navy Seals. In the documentary, the Seal cadets were introduced to "Bertha," a very large log that weighed more than one hundred pounds. The squad of cadets were expected to pick up the log, place it on their shoulders, and then run down the beach with it. Initially, the squad of cadets approached this task as an opportunity to show off their physical strength. But they quickly learned that the task was not to demonstrate their individual physical strength, but rather teamwork. As they approached the task, one of the smaller individuals in the squad found himself placed at the end of the log where managing the immense weight was greater than at other points along the log. The Seal team instructor came over to the squad and pulled a lieutenant aside and asked him what was wrong with the picture he was seeing. He wanted to know why the lieutenant had not rearranged his squad resources to their greatest advantage. Why weren't the smaller, less capable members of the squad placed in the center where they could take advantage of all the larger, more capable members around them? And then he told the lieutenant that he hoped he was never called upon to be a part of a Seal team under the lieutenant's leadership because the instructor was a Chief Petty Officer, and he knew the lieutenant would be the commanding officer. And with leadership like that, he said, he was likely to be placed in a position where he would be killed.

When was the last time you saw the Church of Jesus Christ act like that? And for all the pastors out there, when is the last time you organized your flock according to their strengths? And when was the last time we saw churches across the Nation come together in the strength of Jesus Christ and stand against the lies of Satan?

Yes, I know we organize, we put together statements of faith, we make resolutions, and we hold national days of prayer. But wouldn't you agree that those actions are more like the actions of a country club rather than those of Navy Seals? We need to realize that we are in a spiritual battle and we must prepare as if we are in a spiritual battle. We need to shore up the weak members and take advantage of the strong members. We need to be organized and united under the banner of Jesus Christ. The idea that one church stands alone against the forces of darkness is simply unbelievable.

Would you like to know where I place the blame for the state of the Christian Church in our nation today? I place it directly at *my* feet. I am responsible. I am the one who fails our Father in heaven. I am the one who has not been the lieutenant that He may want me to be. And I am chief among sinners. The only question I have for the rest of the Church is, why are you not in the same place?

I have heard far too many pastors say that they have preached their hearts out and that the people will not respond. Did not Paul say to shake the dust off your feet and to move on? Would the Navy Seals continue to train a failed squad? The Seals take a different approach and encourage those of weak countenance to ring the bell and go home.

Yes, I know the Church is a place of refuge where all may seek shelter. I know there is no condemnation to be found in the Church. But that does not mean the Church is to be weak. Far from it. Jesus demonstrated a strong Church that recognized the lies of Satan and rebuked them. Yes, we are supposed to take in the homeless, the defenseless, the weary, and the poor. But we are also supposed to cultivate homes and teach people to put on the armor of God, and to ensure the weary are well rested, and to help the poor become funded. In other words, we need to be ensuring that the people are living in the strength of God.

Who wants to be a member of a weak military? No veteran or service member that I know. Everyone wants to be on the winning side. And the irony of the situation is, the Church of God **is** the winning side. And we should have members who stand in strength and who can defend those who are not as strong and position them within the battle formations where they are protected from being overwhelmed by the opposition. And we should be portraying a united front across all our congregations against the lies of Satan and the damage he is doing to our land.

So, do we need to plead with God for strength?

> Glory ye in his holy name: let the heart of them rejoice that seek the Lord. Seek the Lord and his strength, seek his face continually. Remember his marvellous works that he hath done, his wonders, and the judgments of his mouth; (1 Chronicles 16:10–12)

We are told that if we glory in His holy name, if we praise Him, honor Him, hold His name in reverence, that our hearts should rejoice in seeking the Lord. We should have great delight in seeking the Lord and joy in seeking His strength. And we should seek His face continuously. Forever. All the time. We should make it a priority in our lives to seek the Lord and His strength. And in doing so, we should remember all the good things He has done for us, His wonderful works and even His judgments against the people and the land.

Sure sounds like a plea to me.

The sixteenth greatest plea ever made: the plea for strength.

THE PLEA FOR WISDOM

Courage and strength fill us with great confidence and a feeling of being able to overcome the world. And indeed, we are even told that we have overcome the world.

> And every spirit that confesseth not that Jesus Christ is come in the flesh is not of God: and this is that spirit of antichrist, whereof ye have heard that it should come; and even now already is it in the world. Ye are of God, little children, and have overcome them: because greater is he that is in you, than he that is in the world. They are of the world: therefore speak they of the world, and the world heareth them. (1 John 4:3–5)

Very plainly, John tells us that those who do not believe, those who do not confess Jesus Christ came as a man, are not of God and are therefore in the world. By contrast, those who do believe, and confess that Jesus Christ came as a man are of God and have overcome those who are in the world because Jesus Christ, who is in you, is greater than Satan, who is in the world.

So, we are told that Jesus Christ is in us with all His strength and all His courage and that we have overcome the world. We are told we are already the victors. But what is this great victory we have won in overcoming the world?

> For this is the love of God, that we keep his commandments: and his commandments are not grievous. For whatsoever is born of God overcometh the world: and

> this is the victory that overcometh the world, even our faith. Who is he that overcometh the world, but he that believeth that Jesus is the Son of God? (1 John 5:3–5)

John tells us that the victory in overcoming the world is our faith. Quite simply, John asked the question, 'Who overcomes the world?' And he answered his question as he asked it, 'Those that believe Jesus is the Son of God'. And then we are supposed to ask the question, "What is belief that Jesus is the Son of God?" And the answer to that is **faith**. John concluded that our belief in Jesus Christ as the Son of God enables us to experience that second birth that Jesus talked to Nicodemus about and inherit the strength and courage of God to overcome the world and gain a great victory, our faith.

But notice I skipped part of the passage. John prefaced his statements by telling us that we should keep God's commandments. He tells us that we return God's love to Him by keeping His commandments. And those commandments will not cause us grief or cause us sorrow. We might debate on whether or not the word *commandments* is used ethically or collectively here, meaning the Ten Commandments as delivered by Moses, or the entirety of moral precepts of Christianity, but for simplicity sake, we will just assume that John was referring to the Mosaic Law of Ten Commandments because that is what would have made the most sense to readers at the time John wrote his letter.

So, before John tells us that those born of God have overcome the world, he tells us first that we need to keep God's commandments and makes a point of telling us that keeping them, while it may not necessarily be easy, will not cause us any pain. Which is a strange thing to say. And it might leave us wondering what that even has to do with overcoming the world. Well hold onto that thought, we will revisit it in a few paragraphs.

What we know so far is that those born of God are filled with His strength and His courage and have overcome the world. We have a great victory that is our faith. We might ask at this point, "So why doesn't the church today act as if they are victorious?" I'm going to contend it is because of our unbelief. Recall that even a tiny amount of faith will move mountains unless it is drowning in a sea of unbelief. But I want to ask a different question here, and that is, "How do we act as victorious?" I know many people think that this is an easy question to answer however, it may be a little more complicated than we think.

At this point, we should recognize that any earthly military would want to have their uniformed service members in exactly this same condition—full of strength and courage, knowing the victory is already theirs before the battle is even engaged, knowing they have overcome the world and that their commander in chief is God. Why they are on God's side and who could possibly be against them? This is exactly the kind of mindset you want to send your troops into battle with. Any military leader will tell you this. Within reason of course.

There are a couple of conditions that you do not want. Of course, you do not want over confidence. You want the troops to fight smartly and within their own limitations. They know what their strengths are and what the enemy's weaknesses are. You do not want your troops acting recklessly and putting the battle plan in jeopardy.

Additionally, you want your troops to follow the rules of war. This might seem strange, and we tend to act as if there are no rules in war, but in reality, there are, and they do serve a purpose. There are times when you are forced take civilian—noncombatant—casualties. And there are times when you need to go to great lengths to avoid them. These are strategic moves that are in place to restrain our barbarianism and to temper the outcomes of war.

More importantly however, you do not want your troops committing war crimes. It is easy for those who hold the victory to rape, pillage, plunder, and ravage the land, to indiscriminately do as they please, wherever they please, and when they please. War crimes put the battle plan at risk and do more to rally the enemy troops while demoralizing your own.

But what about spiritual battles? Does any of this apply to our battles in the world? Well, recall that John told us to return God's love by keeping His commandments? He pointed this out just before telling us that we are victors in overcoming the world. Well, those are the rules of battle. The commandments—God's law—tell us how we are to conduct ourselves in the world. They help to temper our overconfidence in overcoming the world, and they help to prevent us from committing war crimes in overcoming the world.

You may ask if we are capable of committing war crimes in spiritual battles. And I would ask, have our actions ever turned a soul away from Jesus Christ? Has someone ever looked at us and said that he or she would never want to attend our church? Have our actions ever caused shame upon the name of the Lord Jesus Christ? Those are war crimes. Those are times when we act in our own confidence and strength and take matters into our own hands. Sure, we fly the banner of Christ. We proclaim to come in the name of the Lord as we blow up innocent civilians and steal from their lands. We do it all in the name of Jesus Christ. But it is not God's battle plan that we are executing. It is our own.

Should we speak out against the lies of abortion, evolution, the moral decline of our communities, the sheer lack of God-fearing people in our land that has led to a godless revolution in our society? We absolutely should. But where do we draw the line between not bowing down to the golden idols set up by the world, and understanding what Paul was telling us about obeying the government?

> Let every soul be subject unto the higher powers. For there is no power but of God: the powers that be are ordained of God. Whosoever therefore resisteth the power, resisteth the ordinance of God: and they that resist shall receive to themselves damnation. For rulers are not a terror to good works, but to the evil. Wilt thou then not be afraid of the power? do that which is good, and thou shalt have praise of the same: For he is the minister of God to thee for good. But if thou do that which is evil, be afraid; for he beareth not the sword in vain: for he is the minister of God, a revenger to execute wrath upon him that doeth evil. (Romans 13:1–4)

Paul tells us first that we need to be subject to the government because they are ordained of God and are there for good works. I do not know about you, but there are times when I just do not understand the "good works" our governments preform; neither do I understand why so many people champion for a particular politician over another or why many of our politicians are godless people, and yet God allows them to remain in power. But there are two things that I do know. I cannot bow down and worship the idols of humankind. And I need to respect and be subject to the government God has ordained over me.

And those ideals may clash. Exactly how do I follow God's commandments—the rules of war—and stay alive on the battlefield? How do I go to war with those who kill innocent little babies and yet show love and compassion to a young, scared, pregnant teen who has lost all hope in the world? Exactly how do I faithfully execute God's battleplan without taking unnecessary casualties of war?

That requires wisdom. And yes, I mean wisdom, not experience. And no, you do not gain wisdom from experience. That is a misconception we tend to propagate to those we teach. We want those we teach to view us as older and wiser and perhaps full of the wisdom we've gained over the years. This is simply not true. I can list a few dozen people right now who are older than most, have had a lifetime full of experiences, and are even very learned, and yet they lack even the smallest grain of wisdom.

Experience comes from learning from our mistakes. And our mistakes leave a trail of bodies and carnage in their path. Once we have made our mistakes, it is too late to go back and save the souls that we just ran over in our spiritual warfare. And that is not wise.

Wisdom does not come from education either. How in the world can people with multiple PhDs, from Ivy League schools, who graduated at the top of their class with honors, not understand the folly of evolution? Their vaunted intellectual study of the theory is meaningless, a happenstance explanation of the way the universe unfolded. The answer is wisdom. They lack even the smallest grain of wisdom. And Paul said that people in this position are fools: that is, they are court jesters.

So, I need wisdom on the spiritual battlefield in order to carry out the Lord's battle plan, and I cannot gain wisdom from experience, and it doesn't come through education, and without it I'm a fool. Not a very cheery thought. So where do I gain wisdom?

> Only the Lord give thee wisdom and understanding,
> and give thee charge concerning Israel, that thou mayest
> keep the law of the Lord thy God. (1 Chronicles 22:12)

Only the Lord can give you wisdom. Note that wisdom and

understanding help you keep the law. Wisdom and understanding help you in the spiritual battles. And only the Lord can give you wisdom because wisdom comes from the Lord.

> The fear of the Lord is the beginning of wisdom: and the knowledge of the holy is understanding. (Proverbs 9:10)

Wisdom begins with the fear of the Lord. And it is gained by asking for it.

> But let patience have her perfect work, that ye may be perfect and entire, wanting nothing. If any of you lack wisdom, let him ask of God, that giveth to all men liberally, and upbraideth not; and it shall be given him. But let him ask in faith, nothing wavering. For he that wavereth is like a wave of the sea driven with the wind and tossed. (James 1:4–6)

Wisdom is gained from God through a simple request: "God, please grant me the wisdom I need to deal with the situation I am in." Simple, right? Almost sounds too easy, and I am sure there are some people that are wondering, "What's the catch?" And they may be surprised to learn that there is none.

Why would God do this? Why would God, who is all wisdom, simply hand it out to those of His creation who ask for it? I believe the answer is found in the beginning of wisdom. The fear of the Lord is the beginning of wisdom. I must first be aware of the presence of the Lord in my life, and I must fear—that is respect—and honor him before I may even ask for wisdom. It would not make much sense for atheists to ask for wisdom. Atheist are not aware of the presence of God, so they certainly do not fear a god they do not believe in.

The knowledge of the Holy one is understanding. Once I become aware of the presence of the Lord in my life, and suddenly realize I am in the presence of God, I realize I am unworthy, and I cry out for the wisdom of the Lord, and He provides me understanding of Himself, of

His holiness. And He begins to reveal Himself to me. And that is exactly what God wants from all His creation—to reveal Himself to us. But He wants us to help ourselves. He wants us to seek Him out. He wants us to be curious about Him and the kingdom of heaven.

And God knows that, for that to happen, we are going to require wisdom. And so, wisdom is the one thing God will give to anyone who asks. And he will give it in abundance and without prejudice or finding fault. God happily grants wisdom to those who ask for it because He delights in our discovery of Him. He wants us to know Him as well as He knows us. And that is very intimate. The Holy Scriptures tell us that He knows the number of the very hairs on our head.

God wants us to know Him, and He will give us all the wisdom we ask for during our journey to discover Him. But there is a single condition: we must ask in faith. We must begin by believing in Him. The Lord Jesus Christ came to Earth as a testament of God's love for the world. And if we are going to ask Him for wisdom, we must first believe in Him. God will not be mocked. You cannot ask Him for wisdom while not believing in Him in your heart.

We must have wisdom to correctly and effectively execute courage and strength. And wisdom comes from God, whom we need to ask. And that is a plea for wisdom.

The seventeenth greatest plea ever made: the plea for wisdom.

THE PLEA FOR PERSEVERANCE

Even the greatest athletes in the world become tired. We all become tired—military members, young people, old people, and everyone in between. Rest and relaxation are part of the restorative process that is designed into humankind. There is a physical tiredness—a tiredness experienced in our souls—and, for Christians, there is a spiritual tiredness. All parts of our makeup are prone to becoming tired, and when we do not get the rest we need, in our physical bodies, in our souls, and in our spirit, we tend to perform at lower and lower levels and degrade over time. This can lead to depression and eventually hopelessness. We just want to give up.

Paul was aware of this when he wrote the following to the Hebrews:

> Wherefore seeing we also are compassed about with so great a cloud of witnesses, let us lay aside every weight, and the sin which doth so easily beset us, and let us run with patience the race that is set before us, Looking unto Jesus the author and finisher of our faith; who for the joy that was set before him endured the cross, despising the shame, and is set down at the right hand of the throne of God. For consider him that endured such contradiction of sinners against himself, lest ye be wearied and faint in your minds. (Hebrews 12:1–3)

Paul, before a crowd of witnesses, encouraged us to lay aside every weight. To an athlete or physical trainer, this might seem like bad advice. We know that training with weights builds up strength and endurance. Weight training, when properly accomplished, builds up the body and makes us healthier. But Paul was not talking about physical endurance here. He was talking about spiritual endurance.

The weight that Paul was talking about is the weight of the world we carry upon our shoulders. It is what we might be referring to when we speak of someone having a heavy heart. When it comes to the spirit and the soul, the rules of the physical body do not necessarily apply. We do not "train" people who are dealing with the weight of depression by either subjecting them to more depression or regulating the weight of the depression they are already experiencing. And while people may tell stories of going through great hardships and coming out on the other side stronger for it, we would do well to look at what providence helped bring them through the experience.

And the fact that Paul suggested we can "lay aside" these weights would imply that we have the ability to do so. And Paul added to this the weight of our sins that weigh us down and overcome us. And in laying aside this weight, we are to run the race we've been given with patience.

Note that we have had the race "set before us." No one in human history has been able to choose what race he or she wants to run. We do not get to enter the spiritual competition we are most comfortable with; rather the Holy Spirit of God sets the race before to mold us into the people God wants us to be, and not the people we want to be.

This is somewhat contrary to the thinking of the world that would tell you to be your own person, define your own rules, make your own existence. But when we do this, we do it separately from following the path that God would set us on. We do this independently of God.

We might think this unfair. What happened to "free will" and being able to pursue happiness? Well, note how Paul described how we are to run the race set before us. We look to Jesus, keeping our eyes on Him because He is the one performing the work in us. It is He who authored and began the work, and it is He who will eventually finish the work. And Paul even tells us that Jesus Christ endured the race that was set before Him. Recall that Jesus prayed to God the Father three times asking to not have to drink of the cup He had been given. Jesus Christ didn't exactly choose the race He ran, at least not as a man; rather was obedient to God the Father in running it.

And Paul tells us to consider Jesus in running our own race. Why?

Lest we be *wearied* and *faint* in our minds. In other words, lest we be weighed down in our souls. When our emotions overwhelm us, when we experience fear, depression, sadness, loneliness, and hopelessness, it is generally because we are carrying around weights and sins that we have no business carrying.

And the result of that is that we will be weary in the race set before us; we will become faint in the running. Paul is telling us we need to persevere. We need to keep up the good fight. When members of the military become weighed down by the tide of battle, they need renewal; they need to keep their eyes on the prize and persevere in the fight. And the same thing is true for our spiritual battles. How do we persevere in our spiritual battles?

> And take the helmet of salvation, and the sword of the Spirit, which is the word of God: Praying always with all prayer and supplication in the Spirit, and watching thereunto with all perseverance and supplication for all saints; And for me, that utterance may be given unto me, that I may open my mouth boldly, to make known the mystery of the gospel, (Ephesians 6:17–19)

As a young man, I had the good fortune to hear Dr. OS Hawkins preach about the *helmet of salvation*. His description of how our salvation—the helmet—protects us from the fiery darts of Satan was educational to me at the time. He explained how Satan shoots his fiery arrows at our minds, our will, our emotions, our souls. These are the part of us that are most vulnerable. And the helmet that covers our heads protects our minds from those arrows.

How do we persevere in the race set before us? Stay in the word of God. Pray always. Pray with supplication in the Spirit of God. And watching diligently with supplication for all the saints. The plea for perseverance allows us to keep running the race, stay in the fight, and carry on even when we grow weary of the battle.

The eighteenth greatest plea ever made: the plea for perseverance.

THE PLEA OF THE ACCUSED

H ave you ever had to go before a judge? I was called in for jury duty at one point in my life, and I almost made it onto the jury. However, before I was dismissed, I had to answer a litany of questions from both the prosecution and the defense. And there were times during that questioning when I felt as if I was the one being accused and not the defendant who was on trial. Indeed, one of the questions asked was, "Could I put myself into the place of the accused?" As this was a murder trial, I didn't exactly see how I could identity with the accused. I thought, *If they truly want a jury of peers, they need to be interviewing other people accused of murder, and that's not me.*

Accusations in our lives are sharp and hurtful. And we all feel guilty about something. At least we do if we are Christians. There may be atheists or agnostics who feel no guilt, but I will contend that is because their spirits are dead in their sin, and they are not seeking out God.

But our courts are necessary things. We need them to adjudicate the law. And it is no different with God's law. God has a court to adjudicate His law. And we will all stand at that spiritual judgement seat one day. We will either answer the accusations made against us, or else we will enter in the joy of our Lord having been found to have been covered by the blood of the lamb.

And this is not throwing ourselves upon the mercy of the court. Rather it is the court, having mercy, has stepped in and paid our fine, our debt, in full, making us free. The only thing required is believing on Him who paid the price for us—believing that Jesus Christ is the Son of God. And how do I know I will find mercy in that court? Jesus's actions:

Jesus went unto the mount of Olives. And early in the morning he came again into the temple, and all the people came unto him; and he sat down, and taught them. And the scribes and Pharisees brought unto him a woman taken in adultery; and when they had set her in the midst, They say unto him, Master, this woman was taken in adultery, in the very act. Now Moses in the law commanded us, that such should be stoned: but what sayest thou? This they said, tempting him, that they might have to accuse him. But Jesus stooped down, and with his finger wrote on the ground, as though he heard them not. So when they continued asking him, he lifted up himself, and said unto them, He that is without sin among you, let him first cast a stone at her. And again he stooped down, and wrote on the ground. And they which heard it, being convicted by their own conscience, went out one by one, beginning at the eldest, even unto the last: and Jesus was left alone, and the woman standing in the midst. When Jesus had lifted up himself, and saw none but the woman, he said unto her, Woman, where are those thine accusers? hath no man condemned thee? She said, No man, Lord. And Jesus said unto her, Neither do I condemn thee: go, and sin no more. (John 8:1–11)

Here we find Jesus, early in the morning going from the Mount of Olives down to the temple. He was strolling among the olive trees early in the morning, probably praying, perhaps getting ready for what the day would bring. And He headed out to the temple where all the people began to gather around Him. This would have been the multitudes of the city of Jerusalem. And He sat down and began to teach them.

So, Jesus was pretty much minding His own business in the temple. He didn't compel anyone. We are told that the people came to Him. I'm sure that there were no Roman soldiers with spears in the backs of the people forcing them into the temple to see Jesus. These people wanted to be there, and they wanted to hear what Jesus had to say. And I am equally as sure they were free to depart at any time they wished.

If I had been there, I might have been curious and wandered over to see what the great interest in this man was, or I might have just gone about my business for the day. What I would not have done is to suddenly start challenging His teachings in front of all the people. At least not without an invitation to do so.

But this is exactly what the scribes and Pharisees did. And it wasn't enough for them to simply question His teachings, rather, they needed to have an object lesson in order to make their point. And so, when they barged into the temple and confronted Jesus, they were dragging a woman with them. And they sat her down in the midst of the people. And they told Jesus that she had been caught committing adultery. They went as far as to say that she had been taken in the very act, which makes one wonder what the scribes and Pharisees knew in order to be able to find a woman engaged in adultery that early in the morning.

They immediately made an accusation. She had been caught in an adulterous act. Moses and the law commanded that she be stoned. They asked Jesus, "what do you say?" You and I are in the exact same situation as that woman. Satan is dragging us into God's court and accusing us of all our sin and telling God that the law demands we be put to death. So, if you do not think you can identify with this woman, you are wrong. We are all in the same position.

And Jesus didn't say a word to them. Instead, He began to write in the sand with His finger. There are books full of speculation about what Jesus wrote on the ground. Some say he began to write the sins of each of the scribes and Pharisees there. Perhaps He did, but somehow, I believe the accused would have defended themselves, and their protests would have been recorded. And I do not believe people answer accusations with more accusations. But whatever He wrote, I believe that if it had been important, it would have been recorded. And it was not.

What is important is that He posed a bigger problem for them than they had posed for Him. He simply said, "Fine. The law says she should be stoned. If any of you is without sin, go ahead and cast the first stone." This is a very interesting tactic. What judge in any court could impose a fine for speeding who had not violated the speed limit at least once himself or herself? I would guess there are not many. And yet we still enforce the law. The judge, despite being guilty of the exact same crime, will still impose the penalty. At least most will. Some will offer leniency and mercy. So, what was Jesus doing here?

I believe Jesus established that they had brought this woman into His court for judgement. And He was the only one without sin and able to make a fair judgement. The scribes and Pharisees knew they were standing in the presence of the Son of God before leaving that day. And they knew they had best not judge lest they be judged. And so, they withdrew their accusations.

And Jesus did a remarkable thing; he looked at the accused and asked, "Where are your accusers? Isn't there anyone who condemns you?" Of course, when we go to court, we have the right to face our accusers. If we are in court for a traffic ticket, and the officer who issued the citation does not show up, the judge dismisses the case. But the judge generally doesn't ask, the accused, where the officer is. Jesus established Himself as the judge in this story. And He went directly to the accused and asked where her accusers were.

Notice how the woman responded. She said, "No man, Lord." She addressed Jesus Christ as Lord. And Jesus told her that He did not condemn her. He told her to go and sin no more.

Jesus didn't ask her why she hadn't been in the temple listening to His teachings. He didn't talk to her about her motivations for committing adultery. He didn't use her as an object lesson for the people as the scribes and Pharisees had just done. He told her she is not condemned. Her price has been paid. She was free to go. And He asked her to sin no more. What more could the accused plead for? When we are covered by the blood of the Lamb of God and have our sins removed, we are not found in condemnation. What more could we ask for?

When I am asked why God should allow me into the kingdom of God, I should probably respond with the answer Jesus gave Nicodemus: "I believe that Jesus Christ is the Son of God sent into the world because God loves the world." But instead, I like to respond with, "I plead the Blood of the Lamb that was slain for the sins of the world." This may be a slightly more dramatic way of saying the same thing. But the point is that I am covered by the blood. This is usually the end of the conversation for the person who asked. However, I have one additional point I like to add.

And that is that, even if I were to be met at the gates of the kingdom of God by Jesus and He were to tell me that I was not to be allowed in, even after confessing Him Lord, I would still sing, "Praise Him! Praise Him! Praise Him!" as I am led off to hell. And people usually get upset at that and say that I cannot say such a thing.

But here is the truth of the matter: God is God no matter what. And all of creation is for His glory and nothing else. This is *all* about God and *nothing* about me. And just because we presuppose to know the mind of God, we do not. Our purpose is to praise and honor Him no matter what may come. It is He who is the perfect judge, and it is He—and He alone—who will either release or charge the accused. And for that, He is to be praised.

The plea of the accused is to be covered in the Blood of the Lamb that was slain for the sins of the world.

The nineteenth greatest plea ever made: the plea of the accused.

THE PLEA TO NOT BE JUDGED

As we have seen, judgement is a difficult thing. On the one hand, you have the penalty of the law. But on the other, you have the mercy and understanding of the court. There are always mitigating circumstances, right? And of course, there are a host of other factors such as the bias of the judge, whether the judge is having a bad day, or even political pressures the judge may be under from his peers and constituents. Judgement is not an easy task.

However, we ourselves "judge" every single day. Use of our judgement is necessary in making decisions. Sometimes we judge people, and sometimes we judge circumstances. And sometimes we make judgments before we've heard all the facts which would mean that sometimes we make good judgments, and sometimes we make bad judgments.

And as much as we are all judges in our own right, we all must be judged, which puts us all in a quandary because we are told that we should not judge in order to not be judged. And yet, how many of us would want our children to not exercise good judgement when they are off on their own and do not have us around for counsel? Do we not want them to use good judgement when they are with their friends? And do we not want them to use good judgement even when choosing their friends? And how are they to do that if they do not judge the content of their friends' character? Dr. Martin Luther King, Jr. famously stated, *"I have a dream that my four little children will one day live in a nation where they will not be judged by the color of their skin, but by the content of their character."* And I am not sure if he was aware or not, but he identified two types of judgements that sometimes become intertwined.

Dr. King did not make a plea for people to not judge, although he very well could have; rather, he made a plea for the type of judgement that should be applied. Given that we are made in the image of God, and that we have bodies, souls, and spirits, and given that our spirit may be either alive or dead, there are both physical judgements and spiritual judgements in play in our lives. And while Dr. King called for the use of judgement based on content of character, which is not of the spiritual realm, he was indeed saying that physical judgements get us into trouble.

So how do we sort out all these judgements and apply them correctly, and how do we resolve the conflict of not judging in order to not be judged when it is necessary to use good judgement?

We know that we judge after the flesh in the physical realm. We judge others by their appearance, their social mannerisms, their speech, and even their likes and dislikes. And we know that these judgements are useful in helping us to choose friends, spouses, and even business partners and employees.

An employer who interviews a potential employee, is a judge. He or she is making a judgement about the quality and value that person could bring to the company. And there are many things an interviewer is looking for, not the least of which is a good fit for the company. When a person shows up to an interview with unkempt hair and wearing a tank top, cutoff shorts, and flip-flops, the employer has the right and the duty to determine—to judge—whether or not the person exhibits the right look for the company. And if the person is looking to work at the hot dog stand on the beach, perhaps his or her choice of attire is fitting. However, if the person is looking to work in the boardroom of the bank downtown, perhaps the attire is not appropriate. And that is judgement within the physical realm. It is something we deal with all the time.

Dr. King pointed out that our biases sometimes cloud our judgement in the physical realm and that we should, perhaps, shift our judgement from the physical realm to the realm of character, the realm of our souls. Our character is greatly made up of our minds, will, emotions. It consists of the values we have been taught and the values we choose to cling to and practice. It is what animates us. It is that part that links our spirit to our bodies, our soul.

Someone recently told me that the Holy Bible uses the words *soul* and *spirit* interchangeably (it does not), and that there is only one entity, which is known equally as soul or spirit. In other words, you have a soul, and that *is* your spirit, or you have a spirit and that *is* your soul. They are one in the same. Two words used to refer to one thing. This may sound great, but it doesn't work for our judgements.

Jesus described a second birth, a new life, to Nicodemus. And without that re-birth, Jesus said we are dead. And He made it clear that one life is from water—is physical, and one is from spirit—it is spiritual in nature. And knowing this, we realize that we deal with people who are dead in spirit all the time. In other words, there are non-believers in the world whose spirits are dead. And yet we judge them on the content of their character. Where does that character come from? It is not a part of their physical bodies. And if their spirits are dead, they cannot exhibit much character. Character exists within our souls. And people with dead spirits can have good character, and, unfortunately, people with alive spirits can have bad character. But either way, people still have both soul and spirit—two separate entities, both very real and part of our makeup.

When we judge people by the content of their character, we may use clues or evidence from the physical world. When our potential employee came in for the interview, we may have noticed evidence of drug use. Perhaps her clothing smelled of marijuana smoke, or perhaps she had a joint in her hand, or maybe her clothing was decorated with symbols or paraphernalia that identified her with drug use or a drug culture. These would all be physical evidence of a choice of character: being a drug addict is what I choose to be and is part of my character. And not being a drug addict is also a choice of character. And judging whether a company wants to hire a drug addict is perfectly reasonable and a legitimate judgement of character to make. That is judgement within the realm of the soul, and we deal with it all the time.

Judgement of the spirit is a judgment for all eternity. Have you ever known someone who was a nice, well-dressed person, that had good moral values, that was just evil? Why is that? Abortion is evil. It is just morally and ethically wrong to rip a human being from its mother's womb and leave them to die. And yet there are people who champion the cause and perform the killing. These people might otherwise be seemingly decent people, not stealing from others, obeying the traffic laws, keeping their lawn neat and their house clean, seemingly of good character. And yet they are fine with killing an innocent human baby in its mother's womb.

Why is that? I would contend that it is because their dead spirit presents an opportunity for Satan's demons to take control. They exhibit evilness because evil itself has come and set up shop in their lives. It is their spirit that is dead and without God. There are many examples of this throughout history. Serial killers, dictators, and war criminals. People that have acted with a hatred and evilness that defies all common sense and decency. All because they have allowed their dead spirits to be a home to demons.

And yes, we tend to judge these people in the spirit also, generally wishing them dead physically as well as spiritually. However, that wish is a fatal one for all of eternity. It seals their fate without ever having a second chance to know and experience God. Judging in the spirit is final.

Now that we've seen how we judge in our bodies, our souls, and our spirit, we can begin to understand how we fit all of it together to be good, fair, impartial judges in our lives. And it begins with mercy:

> Be ye therefore merciful, as your Father also is merciful. Judge not, and ye shall not be judged: condemn not, and ye shall not be condemned: forgive, and ye shall be forgiven: Give, and it shall be given unto you; good measure, pressed down, and shaken together, and running over, shall men give into your bosom. For with the same measure that ye mete withal it shall be measured to you again. (Luke 6:36–38)

Firstly, we are told to be merciful in the exact same way that God the Father is merciful. When we judge, we need to judge from a position of mercy and understanding. God does not start from a position of condemnation in our lives. God starts from a position of mercy and love. And the first thing we need to do to temper our biases and prejudices in our judgements, is to start from a place of mercy.

Secondly, we are not told that we cannot judge, but rather that we should not judge in order to not be judged. And that is not intentionally a tongue twister. We have already seen that we need to exercise good judgement in our lives. Does that automatically mean that we will be judged? I believe there is evidence of that in our world. At the same time the employer is judging the potential employee, the potential employee is judging the potential employer. Does that mean we stop making judgements? Of course not. Good judgements are still required in our lives.

What we are being told here is that we should not be judgmental, which is defined as making excessively harsh and critical judgements based upon some perceived moral high ground. And we know this because of the very next thing we are told is: "condemn not, and ye shall not be condemned." When we are judgmental, as opposed to exercising good judgement, we are quick to condemn and slow to forgive.

I can use good judgement without being judgmental in my actions. I may use good judgement by explaining to the person in the interview that the company has a dress code and that he will not be allowed in the building in a tank top, cutoff shorts, and flip-flops. I am not being judgmental of the person for his choice of attire, I am not condemning him for the way he dressed for the interview. But I may suggest that, without mitigating circumstances, for which he can be forgiven, that he exercised poor judgement. And yes, I know that might be a little confusing— exercising good judgement without being judgmental. But that is why judgement is a difficult thing.

> Then spake Jesus again unto them, saying, I am the light of the world: he that followeth me shall not walk in darkness, but shall have the light of life. The Pharisees therefore said unto him, Thou bearest record of thyself; thy record is not true. Jesus answered and said unto them, Though I bear record of myself, yet my record is true: for I know whence I came, and whither I go; but ye cannot tell whence I come, and whither I go. Ye judge after the flesh; I judge no man. And yet if I judge, my judgment is true: for I am not alone, but I and the Father that sent me. (John 8:12–16)

Jesus told the people that He is the light of the world and that those who follow Him would not walk in darkness. This is a bold statement that only God could make. And immediately the Pharisees were judgmental. How do I know the Pharisees were judgmental in their response? Because Jesus said that they were.

If I tell you that I am a great cook, I am only as credible to the extent to which you believe me. You would have every right to be skeptical because we cannot defend our own honor. That statement is hollow and without substance. However, if a crowd of people came to you and started telling you how wonderful my cooking was, and assuming I had not bribed them to say so, then you might begin to wonder just how good my cooking really was. There is something about a crowd of witnesses that offers credibility to our defense. Which is why they say that only a fool has himself for a lawyer in a trial. By the way, I'm not a great cook, so maybe that was a bad example.

And this is exactly the argument that the Pharisees made to Jesus: "You are telling us you are the light of the world? We do not believe you. It's not true." The Pharisees told Jesus that He could not testify on His own behalf and expect them to believe Him.

But God can testify on His own behalf. And the Creator can testify on His own behalf to the creation. Jesus corrected the Pharisees on this point, and then He pointed out the flaw in their approach. They were being judgmental. They were judging after the flesh. Jesus said that He judges no man. That would be after the flesh. But if He does judge, that would be after the spirit, His judgement is true because it is made along with God the Father.

No one wants to be judged, but we all need to exercise good judgement. And the only way we are going to arrive at that point in our lives is by understanding mercy, condemnation, and forgiveness as God would have us understand them. And that needs to start with a plea.

The twentieth greatest plea ever made: the plea to not be judged.

THE PLEA TO LEARN

People are curious just as Nicodemus was curious when he came to Jesus in the night seeking the kingdom of God. Curious people learn things, and when we learn, we believe we have become wise, but the Bible warns us that we may become as fools:

> Because that, when they knew God, they glorified him not as God, neither were thankful; but became vain in their imaginations, and their foolish heart was darkened. Professing themselves to be wise, they became fools, And changed the glory of the uncorruptible God into an image made like to corruptible man, and to birds, and fourfooted beasts, and creeping things. (Romans 1:21–23)

When we are curious; and begin to learn about the world around us, we learn of God. Because He manifests Himself in His creation. But when we do not recognize God for who He is—as our Creator—then we begin to believe the lies of Satan and become vain, proud, and conceited in our own imaginations. Our foolish hearts are darkened. And in our vanity, we then profess ourselves to be wise. But God says we are as fools. And we then change the glory of God—His creation—into something made in the likeness of ourselves; and the fowl of the air and the beasts of the field and even the insects that crawl upon the Earth.

More than two thousand years ago, Paul predicted the theory of evolution. Long before Charles Darwin ever traveled to the Galapagos Islands and began to develop the theory of evolution, Paul wrote in his letter to the Romans that this was the path mankind was bound to take.

Paul knew that, if we ever denied the Creator, we would begin to look to creation itself as our god.

But God does want us to learn. He wants us to study the creation. God is not against science. He is not against biology, geology, or physics. God is the author of all science. God created a great big universe to demonstrate His majesty and His glory and His greatness. God wants us to know Him, and one way we know God is through the study of His creation. He commanded us to have dominion, control, and authority over all the Earth. And it is difficult to have authority over something you have no understanding of. And so, there is a need to learn.

The problem comes when we start believing the lies of Satan and take God out of the picture. Without God, we are left with a creation with no creator. And that is where things start to break down. Because now we must profess ourselves wise in order to explain a creation without a creator.

God delights in our knowing Him. And the more we learn about His creation, both here on Earth and in the entire universe, the more we learn of His majesty. And we should give Him glory for that.

God would never have given us dominion over something that we were not able to handle. It would be folly to believe that God would sit in heaven and tell the angels in heaven to watch as humankind discovered fossil fuels, built cities and highways and gasoline powered engines, and then used it all to destroy the Earth. God knew exactly what He was doing when He gave us authority over the Earth and what we would do with that authority. And if God thought there was going to be a problem with our exercising that authority, He would have done what any good parent would do; He would have protected us.

There are people who are completely terrified of the future. They believe the Earth is doomed because of Global Climate Change, nuclear war, the overpopulation of the world and running out of food and water, but this is all pure folly to God. These people live in fear because they have no God. And without God, there is no hope, no faith, and no light.

Christians, know what the end of this world will hold because God gave us a peek into His great plan in the book of Revelation and we have hope that Jesus Christ is victorious, and that God is in control.

But we need to learn in the spirit as well as in the physical world. One day the disciples came to Jesus and pleaded with Him to teach them to pray. This one simple act of learning opens a door to communication with God. It is how we learn though communication with our Creator:

> And it came to pass, that, as he was praying in a certain place, when he ceased, one of his disciples said unto him, Lord, teach us to pray, as John also taught his disciples. And he said unto them, When ye pray, say, Our Father which art in heaven, Hallowed be thy name. Thy kingdom come. Thy will be done, as in heaven, so in earth. Give us day by day our daily bread. And forgive us our sins; for we also forgive every one that is indebted to us. And lead us not into temptation; but deliver us from evil. (Luke 11:1–4)

Jesus taught His disciples, that, when they pray, they should approach God as Father. This paints a picture of an earthly child who wants to learn from an earthly father. Most of my interests in life, most of my desires to learn about various disciplines and tradecrafts, all were either heavily influenced or came from my father.

God is no different than an earthly father in this regard. The heavenly Father, the Father in heaven in our prayers, wants us to know His interests and His passions as well. He wants to be a good influence in our lives, and He wants us to grow and to learn.

We are to praise the name of our Father. Holy is His name. Children are meant to be proud of their parents. This is lacking in today's world. And it is certainly lacking in the spiritual world. When I was in grade school, we would go before the class and tell all our classmates what our fathers and mothers did for a living. And everyone wanted to paint a larger-than-life picture of their parents. They wanted to portray their parents as the most important people on Earth with the most important jobs. Imagine what the world would be like if we were to tell of the importance of our heavenly Father and what an important job He has in holding all of creation in the palm of His hand and how He cares for us and how not even a sparrow falls from the sky or a blade of grass withers on the ground that He is not aware of. What do you think the other students in the class would think?

And imagine their awe and surprise when they learn that they too can be part of the same family. They can call God in heaven Father.

We are to acknowledge His providence. We are to pray for His kingdom to come to Earth and for His will to be done just as it is in heaven.

My parents were great providers. We never lacked for food, clothing, or shelter. They taught us children not only about the world, but also about Jesus Christ and His provision in our lives. We prayed before every meal. We acknowledged that it was God who sustained us and carried us through. And we had more toys than we ever deserved. My parents kept us interested in the world around us. But it was my parents who provided, not us children. Even when we had chores to do and were paid for those chores, that money came from the wealth of my mom and dad.

Our heavenly Father wants the same for all of us, but we fail to acknowledge that it is His provision in our lives that sustains us. It is His kingdom that provides for us. And it is His will that sustains our lives and our happiness. When we acknowledge the provision of God in our lives, our world changes and our priorities become realigned from earthly things to heavenly things.

My mom is a such great cook that I insisted that my wife learn her recipes and techniques. And even today, when my wife bakes a pie for a neighbor or a friend, using my mom's recipe of course, she is told that it is the best pie they have ever had in their lives. There were times when Mom would serve something that we children were not quite so fond of—maybe a squash casserole—and we would not want to eat it. But my parents would insist that we eat it. We learned to be thankful for our food and the nourishment that we had, and we never once went hungry.

God in heaven is the same way. He wants us to come to the dinner table prepared to eat what He has to serve. And we are to do that daily. He said we are to ask "give us day by day". Recall that we are creatures of replenishment. We need to constantly be renewed. God wants us to return to His table every day and be fed with the bread He has prepared for us. I believe this inherent design condition is to keep us dependent upon Him. God does not want us to eat once, be filled, and leave the dinner table to never think about Him again. He wants to see us back at the next mealtime.

Another thing our family routinely did as we sat around the dinner table besides pray and eat the great food that Mom served, was to share. We would talk about how we were doing in school, or what television shows we would watch that night, or what projects we had going on. More so than perhaps any other time, we would share around the family dinner table.

God wants us to come to the dinner table ready to share. He wants to know how our day is going. He wants to know our struggles and our pains. And He wants to share with us. Jesus, here on Earth, shared of the Father in heaven many times over meals. God wants us to come to the dinner table and share with Him, and He wants to share with us.

One thing that was not allowed around our dinner table was unwarranted accusations. My parents had little tolerance for an unforgiving heart. And many times, when I was unforgiving, I would be reminded of my own sins against my parents and how I had been forgiven.

It is the same at God's table. We are to seek God's forgiveness and to forgive others in kind. No one wants to eat at the dinner table with someone who has an unforgiving heart. God wants all to be welcome at His table, so He does not want unforgiving hearts at the table. And since we are creatures of sin, there must be continuous forgiveness. God expects us to continuously seek forgiveness and to offer forgiveness.

And lastly, we are to ask for God's protection. My parents were fiercely protective of us children. They wanted to know where we were, who we were with, and how long we expected to be there. They wanted to know who was supervising us and what authority would be exercised by that supervision. They were protective of their children. My parents believed they had a responsibility as parents, and they strove to execute that responsibility with soberness and with due diligence.

God in heaven is the same way. He wants to protect His children. And when we pray, we are to acknowledge that He is our protector and keeper. He keeps us from evil. A lot of times we fall prey to the lies of Satan simply because we do not pray to be delivered from evil. If we were more diligent about praying, and asking to be delivered from evil, I believe we would be living in a different country and a different world. If we would simply ask the Father in heaven to deliver us from evil, then the next time Satan tried to snare us with his lies, God would immediately step in and tell Satan that we are His children and under His protection and that he needs to move off.

When we learn to pray, we learn to commune with God. And when we learn to commune with God we begin to learn about God's great plan, all His creation, and how much He loves us. And that begins to change our world as we explore His riches and His depths. Since He is an infinite God and has placed us in an infinite universe, we're going to need an eternity of learning. But it all begins with a plea, teach us to pray.

The twenty-first greatest plea to ever be made: the plea to learn.

THE PLEA TO NOT BE LOST

When I learned to drive, the Global Positioning System (GPS) did not exist. The first GPS system did not appear as a built-in system in an automobile until 1990. For more than a decade, I drove around with a stack of maps and an atlas in my car. Whenever I traveled to someplace new, I had a habit of stopping and buying the latest-edition maps for that location because not only did I not want to be lost, there were also times when I could not afford to be lost. People generally do not want to wander around lost for very long.

All of that changed with the introduction of the GPS. Now the maps are digital and automatically downloaded for me. And today, not only is the GPS built right into my car, it will also talk to me and give me directional accuracy down to tens of feet, something the old paper maps could never do. Using the old paper maps, I would miss turns on occasion, misread street signs, and end up in places I never wanted to be. That almost never happens today. And if I really mess things up, the GPS is smart; it works hard to get me back on track. It tells me exactly where I need to go in order to get to where I want to be.

The same thing is true in our spiritual lives. We do not want to be lost spiritually. We want to know where we are and where we are going. Oftentimes we want to travel by the most efficient path possible. Fortunately for us, we have a spiritual GPS:

> But he turned, and said unto Peter, Get thee behind me, Satan: thou art an offence unto me: for thou savourest not the things that be of God, but those that be of men. Then said Jesus unto his disciples, If any man will come after me, let him deny himself, and take up his cross, and

follow me. For whosoever will save his life shall lose it: and whosoever will lose his life for my sake shall find it. (Matthew 16:23–25)

Peter once tried to derail the course of Jesus Christ. But Jesus immediately recognized his effort as bad directions. Jesus knew His directions were true, His compass was accurate, and His map was sure. And because of this, He stayed on course.

But then he turned to his disciples and told them how to never be lost again as well. And in doing so He revealed that He is indeed our GPS. But there are some rules to follow. As with any technology, the effectiveness of the tool is bound up in how you use it.

When I was learning to fly, there came a point when we practiced instrument training. Imagine having to drive your car with no way to see the road in front of you or behind you and no way of being able to see traffic around you—no windshield, no mirrors, just the instrument panel in front of you and instructions coming from your radio.

This is what instrument flying is like. You must rely solely on the instruments in the plane and radio communications from Air Traffic Control to make your way through a three-dimensional space. If you do not believe that makes things harder, have someone tightly blindfold you and put you on a roller coaster. Just try to anticipate where the next turn, climb, or drop will take place. And do that while determining speed.

When we were practicing flying by instruments, my instructor would often say, "My plane." This indicated I was no longer the one in control of the plane. She would have me drop the hood, a method of blindfolding yourself in the plane so that you can no longer see outside of the plane or inside of the plane, I could not see the instrument panel or what the instructor was doing. And she would then fly the plane in an erratic manner. She would stall the plane, pitch it over on its side, put it into a dive, turn it off course, or change the speed. Sometimes all at once. The plane would no longer be where I knew it to be when I turned it over to her. And then she would suddenly say, "Your plane!" I was to now raise the hood so that I could see just the instrument panel but not outside of the plane. And I was expected to safely fly the plane at that point.

I was so quick at scanning the instrument panel and assessing the position of the plane that, at times, she would feign disgust and complain that I was just too good at the exercise. But I would just tell her that I would ignore all the confusing inputs my body was giving me while blindfolded and instead prepare myself mentally for scanning the instrument panel when the time came for using the information to get the plane back under control and on course.

This is what Jesus means when He says that, to follow Him you must deny yourself. He wants you to blindfold yourself to all the inputs of the world. He wants you to allow Him to take control of your life. You are to shut out all the chaos, temptation, and sin of the world and concentrate on Jesus. Jesus is now your instrument panel. What comes from the world is misleading and will take you off course. But as long as you deny the erroneous information, and solely trust in your instruments, you will be okay. Jesus wants us to rely solely on Him and His guidance, and that means denying the bad navigation information we get from the world.

Next, Jesus tells us that we must take up our cross. If you are going to follow Jesus, you are going to have a cross. Jesus doesn't want us outpacing Him, and since He is carrying a cross, He wants us to carry a cross as well in order to stay right in step with Him. Carrying a cross is a constant reminder of where we are going and the path we must walk to get there. And carrying a cross helps keep us on course by regulating our steps and keeping us from wandering off the path Jesus would have us follow.

If we trust Jesus, deny ourselves, and take up our cross, the rest is easy. We just follow Him. We walk where He walks, we step where He steps: His footprints become our guide. Jesus becomes our GPS. And we never need be lost again. Should we stray and become lost, the Bible tells us that Jesus is aware and will stop and track us down and bring us back into the fold.

Jesus said that, if we lose our life for His sake, meaning give up trying to navigate on our own and trust in Him, we will find life—spiritual life in abundance in the kingdom of God. But if we try to save our lives, meaning go it alone without Jesus and under our own navigation, we will lose our spiritual lives and spend an eternity in hell. If we ignore the only instrument of guidance that can keep us on course and take us safely home, and follow all the ways of the world, we will surely end up crashing the plane:

Thomas saith unto him, Lord, we know not whither thou goest; and how can we know the way? Jesus saith unto him, I am the way, the truth, and the life: no man cometh unto the Father, but by me. If ye had known me, ye should have known my Father also: and from henceforth ye know him, and have seen him. (John 14:5–7)

Spiritually, Jesus Christ is the only GPS that can keep us on track here on Earth while guiding us to the kingdom of God. There is no other way to come to the Father in heaven except by the guidance and navigation of Jesus Christ. He is designed as the instrument panel of your life. You can ignore the instrument panel and see all the world has to show you, and you will end up spiritually blind. Or you can become blind to the world and see what Jesus has to show you on the instrument panel of your life.

Jesus Christ is the only GPS that can direct you safely through life. He will tell you when your life is off course and what you must do to get back on course. He will guide you to the Father in heaven. And He will keep you safe enroute and not allow you to crash. This does not mean that we do not experience stormy weather. We do. Sometimes the flight is full of rough air that shake and buffet the plane about in the sky. There will be storms in our path, but Jesus Christ is the only hope for navigating those storms and making it safely though. Belief in Jesus Christ will ensure we are not lost but know the way to the kingdom of God.

No one wants to be lost, and it is so much sweeter to be found. How can you know the way? Be like Thomas and plead "Lord, how can we know the way?"

The twenty-second greatest plea ever made: the plea to not be lost.

THE GREATEST PLEA
NEVER MADE

> And, behold, one of them which were with Jesus stretched out his hand, and drew his sword, and struck a servant of the high priest's, and smote off his ear. Then said Jesus unto him, Put up again thy sword into his place: for all they that take the sword shall perish with the sword. Thinkest thou that I cannot now pray to my Father, and he shall presently give me more than twelve legions of angels? But how then shall the scriptures be fulfilled, that thus it must be? (Matthew 26:51–54)

In this passage from Matthew, we find Jesus in the garden of Gethsemane with his disciples, the very men chosen by Him three years earlier. In just a few hours He would be falsely accused, tried before the most unjust court in human history, horribly beaten and scourged, and nailed to a cross where He would give up His life for all of humanity. Before that happens, He must be arrested; and at the moment in time described in this passage, He voluntarily allows soldiers to restrain Him and a mob to demand His trial and execution.

As the crowd advanced to lay hold of Jesus, one of the chosen men (revealed as Simon Peter in the account given in John 18:10–13) draws his sword and cuts off the ear of the servant of the high priest. Which is a very bold move for Peter. The crowd that had arrived to take Jesus is described as a "great multitude" in the Gospel of Mark. We are told that they had swords and staves. And we know they would have brought a Roman guard with them. So, for Peter to brashly draw his sword and strike out at someone from the crowd before him was very daring indeed. But from Peter's perspective he had seen Jesus do amazing things over the past three years. Peter had seen miraculous things. Things that were unexplainable by human reasoning. And when asked by Jesus who He—Jesus—was, it was Peter that immediately answered, "Thou art the Christ" (Mark 8:29). Peter was probably feeling very confident, perhaps even invincible. After all, he had the messiah on his side.

I believe Peter made a terrible mistake in these actions. A mistake easily made by those caught up in a disaster requiring an immediate response. Peter's mistake was that he did not seem to have a battle plan. His sword did not kill, rather it simply landed a glancing blow to the side of the head managing to cut off an ear. Neither do we see any of the other disciples join in the battle. As far as we know, Peter may have been the only one of the disciples who carried a sword. Peter had failed to coordinate his response and to make sure that the rest of the disciples understood the plan of action.

Oftentimes people simply react to a crisis within their lives without considering the consequences. They fail to check with those around them who could possibly offer help and advice. They ignore their support group that is usually right there with them watching the whole disaster unfold. Often, people make bad situations worse by reacting in a crisis without a plan, without counsel, and without a support group that can join in battling the adversity and help ensure victory.

Peter made one other critical error that we may learn an important lesson from. Peter failed to check with the on-scene authority before acting. Jesus Christ, God in the flesh, was standing right there beside him and Peter failed to stop and recognize the Master. Peter had seen Jesus perform miracles and he knew that if he kept his eyes on Jesus he could walk on water (Matthew 14:29). But caught up in the crisis he was now facing, Peter reacted without first receiving his battle orders from the one who was in control of the situation.

The person in control of a disaster is always the calm, measured, and decisive person. This is usually a professional, a fire fighter, police officer, or other first responder; but it does not always have to be. It could be anyone in your nearby support group that has faced the same or similar situation in the past. It could be the person with the experience and understanding to help guide you to the most successful outcome. This person will always be recognizable in your life, and it would always be wise to seek their advice before reacting to a crisis in your life.

If you are a disciple of Jesus Christ, then you already know who your on-scene authority is. Just as He was there in the garden with Peter and the other disciples when the crisis came, so He is there with you when you face a crisis in your own life. Whenever you find yourself face to face with an angry mob armed with swords and staves, just remember that God in the flesh, Jesus Christ, is standing right there with you and He has faced the situation before. Jesus Christ holds all authority in all of creation (see Colossians 1:16) and we simply need to recognize Him as the authority in our lives whenever we face difficulties.

Jesus, who really was in control of the crisis in the garden, told Peter to cease with his attack and to put his sword back into its sheath. It was Jesus who was in control, not Peter, not the other disciples, and not even the angry mob, Jesus commanded all authority, and it was His plan that was being carried out. A plan written before the world began. A plan that had been unfolding for more than four thousand years. A plan that would have never been devised by man and could have only come from God Himself. A perfect plan written by Him, for Him, and that He alone could execute. A plan devised to bring Him all honor, and all glory, and all praise. And a plan that would result in the name of Jesus Christ being exalted above every name (Philippians 2:8–10).

And Jesus, being completely in control, does a very curious thing here. He asks Peter a question. Jesus looks at Peter and basically says, "Don't you think I could cry out to God the Father right now and He would provide more than twelve legions of angels?" We need to recall at this point that it was only an hour or so earlier that Jesus was earnestly pleading with God the Father to not have to drink of this cup. While Peter may have slept through those prayers, Matthew certainly was aware of them as he recorded them in his gospel. Jesus, who had pleaded with God the Father to not have to go to His death on the cross, now told Peter with all certainty that God the Father would provide more than twelve legions of angels if He would just ask.

A legion of Roman soldiers numbered between four thousand and six thousand men. I tend to believe God would always provide forces in full strength when answering a cry for help from His Son, so we should just assume that Jesus was telling Peter that more than seventy-two thousand angels were standing ready to appear before Him if He would but cry out for help.

What we need understand here is the awesome force Jesus was describing to Peter that He had available at His disposal. In II Kings 19:35 an angel of the Lord killed one hundred eighty-five thousand Assyrian soldiers in a night. One angel of the Lord took on one hundred eighty-five thousand trained and battle-hardened soldiers and left every single one of them dead in a very few short hours. Most likely without even trying hard. Angels are mighty and fearsome creations and every single time one shows up before people, the Bible records that the people were very afraid. So afraid that often they would bow down before the angel as if in worship; prompting the angel to command the people to not worship them as they were not God. And if we simply apply the math to the scenario given by Jesus Christ to Peter in the garden, we would have more than seventy-two thousand angels each one of which would be capable of killing one hundred eighty-five thousand battle-hardened soldiers in a couple of hours resulting in a force capable of wiping out thirteen billion three hundred twenty million people in a single night. That is much more than the population of the entire earth today.

We should consider that fact very carefully. Jesus was essentially telling Peter that he commanded an army of angels capable of ending the Earth in a single night. All of humanity erased from existence in the space of a few hours. An overwhelming force which the world would not be able to respond to. The only thing Jesus had to do to ensure the end of humanity was to make one simple plea for help to God the Father.

Jesus Christ *did not* make that plea. Rather he asked Peter a second question. Jesus told Peter that He *could* ask for more than twelve legions of angels, guaranteeing the destruction of all of humanity, but, if He were to do that, then how would the scriptures be fulfilled? How can the Word of God stand true if Jesus Christ is not *The Truth*? Jesus asserts that He must not make that plea in order for the scriptures—the Word of God—to be proven true.

Jesus did not cry out for help. He did not plead with God the Father for twelve legions of angels. Jesus chose to see the needs of others while understanding the consequences of not meeting His own needs. And at that moment in time, God, the creator of the universe, the Lord of lords, the King of kings, the Alpha and the Omega, humbled Himself and bowed before the creation. He allowed Himself to be bound and led away to the cross for you and for me and for all of humanity across all of time. Jesus Christ, the Son of the Living God, the Messiah, a part of the triune Deity who created all, chose *not* to make a plea.

Jesus Christ, who had made the blind to see, the lame to walk, the deaf to hear, and the dumb to talk, did not consider His own need to cry out for help. Jesus Christ, who had walked on water, turned water into wine, and fed more than five thousand people with nothing more than a boy's lunch basket, chose to look across time and see the needs of all of humanity and considered humanities needs greater than His own.

Jesus Christ, who had healed the sick and raised the dead to life, allowed His love for us—the creation made in His perfect image—to be made manifest in the laying down of His life so that we could live eternally with Him.

The greatest plea never made was when Jesus chose *not* to call upon more than twelve legions of angels, but rather chose to accept God's great plan and go to His death on the cross in order to save you and me. God's great plan of salvation was born out of the greatest plea never made.

THE CRIES OF THE WORLD

The world today is in as much of a crisis as it has ever been in. Two thousand years ago the world saw nations that wanted to conquer and saw criminals that wanted nothing but their own gain. Two thousand years ago the world saw pestilence and lepers who sat outside of the city gates. And two thousand years ago, the world saw natural disasters like earthquakes and volcanos that threatened cities and outlying lands.

Two thousand years ago, people could lose their lives to lions or bears on the road to Rome. They could end up stranded in the desert on a journey. Two thousand years ago, members of law enforcement were just as likely to take people's lives as murderers. Two thousand years ago, if an earthquake were to open all the prison doors a jailer was responsible for guarding, that jailer may very well have decided to take his own life rather than face the wrath of his superiors.

And yet today we seem to want to believe that things are much, much worse. We say that crime is the worst it has ever been. We watch videos of thieves brazenly breaking into stores and smashing cases and stealing merchandise. But how many thieves do we see hanging on crosses outside of our towns?

We live in fear of the weather. We worry that hurricanes and tornados and melting polar ice caps are going to destroy the world. We hold global climate accords and try to convince each other that if every nation does not do some part, the world will end.

We scream about a planet and a people in peril. And we are as divided as ever on issues of governance as we struggle for dominance in the political arena. We are lost spiritually as well. Our churches, synagogues, and temples do not garner the respect and attendance that they did just a few decades ago.

But if we were to take all our problems and calamities and set them aside for a moment, perhaps we could turn our pleas for help to God and in doing so find something much richer and much more satisfying.

What if we were to develop a curiosity, a hunger, an unquenchable thirst to know God? A plea of curiosity to see the kingdom of God would lead us to Jesus.

Finding Jesus, we would become aware of our sin. Would that cause us to issue a plea for mercy? Would we cry out to God to have mercy on us? If we did, we would find that God grants mercy.

Would finding mercy lead us to question our unbelief and cause us to plea for help in our unbelief? Because we would find that help in Jesus Christ.

Would we then not want to be forgotten in the kingdom of God? Would we plead with Jesus to be remembered? Jesus remembers all who come to Him in faith.

Would being remembered of God help us find hope? Because Jesus offers hope to the world.

And finding hope, would we then have a reason to live and want to plead for life? Jesus Christ is the only one who offers life, and life more abundant than we can ever imagine.

With that newfound life, would we want to find salvation? Would we plead to be saved? Only Jesus Christ can save us. He is the way, the truth, and the life. And no person comes to the Father but by Him.

Finding ourselves with a path to the kingdom of God, would we plead to not be hindered? We would find that, if we believe that Jesus Christ is the Son of God, the Lamb that was slain for the sins of the world, nothing can hinder us in coming to God.

And finding God, would we plead to know the truth? Because only Jesus Christ is truth. And when we know the truth, the truth will set us free.

In finding truth in God, would we plead to know God more? Would we seek His face constantly and want to spend time with Him?

As we grow to know God, would we then plead for His peace in our lives? We would find that only Jesus provides the peace that passes all understanding.

And if we were to experience God's peace in our lives, would we then plead to experience His joy? Because only Jesus Christ came that our joy might be full.

Experiencing the joy of God, would we plead to be immersed in His love? Because God is love, and he gave of His only begotten Son that we might have life with Him.

And finding ourselves immersed in His love, would we then plead to be fed at His table? Jesus Christ is the bread of life. And whoever eats at His table and drinks of His cup will never hunger or thirst again.

Finding ourselves no longer hungry or thirsty, would we plead for the courage to face the world? Because we would find that Jesus has overcome the world.

And as we grew in courage, would we plead for His strength to be able to fight the battles before us? We would find that Jesus is greater in us, that he who is in the world.

The more we experienced of His victories in our lives, would we plead for wisdom in order to remain humble servants? God grants wisdom to all men liberally.

The more we grew in wisdom, would we plead for perseverance to be able to complete the journey? We would find that the yoke that Jesus asks us to bear is easy and His burden is light.

And as we walked along that journey, would we plead to not be among the accused? Jesus did not come into the world to condemn the world, but rather to save the world.

Not being among the accused, would we plead to not be judged? We would find that if we are covered by the Blood of the Lamb, our sins are forgiven, and our debt has been paid.

Finding ourselves free of condemnation and shame, would we plead to learn more and more about Jesus? We would find that those who sit at His feet will discover Him.

And then finding an infinite and Holy God, would we plead for guidance that we may not be lost in our journey but would always be in the footsteps of our Lord Jesus Christ?

It takes a lifetime to accomplish these twenty-two simple pleas. But also, these twenty-two simple pleas can change our lives, change our country, and change the world around us were we to all join in pursuing them together.

Those are the greatest pleas ever made by mankind. The plea to know God. And the pleas that are answered with "He that believeth on him is not condemned: but he that believeth not is condemned already, because he hath not believed in the name of the only begotten Son of God." Believe in Jesus Christ as Lord, Savior, the Messiah sent forth by God as the payment for the sins of the world.

We would fill a huge library with hundreds of books if we were to chronicle all the wars, tribulations, calamities, hardships, sorrows, heartaches, injustices, inequities, disasters, sickness, disease, hate, pain, and suffering in the world today. However, thankfully, there is just one book needed for the answers to every single one of those problems and any others humankind may not have yet encountered: the Holy Bible, the Word of God.

If we were to take up the Holy Bible and begin to plead with God for answers to all our problems, I believe He would answer us.

> And the Lord appeared to Solomon by night, and said unto him, I have heard thy prayer, and have chosen this place to myself for an house of sacrifice. If I shut up heaven that there be no rain, or if I command the locusts to devour the land, or if I send pestilence among my people; If my people, which are called by my name, shall humble themselves, and pray, and seek my face, and turn from their wicked ways; then will I hear from heaven, and will forgive their sin, and will heal their land. Now mine eyes shall be open, and mine ears attent unto the prayer that is made in this place. (2 Chronicles 7:12–15)

Most people who quote these verses usually begin with verse 14, which begins with "If my people …" This leaves off a very significant part of the passage. Notice in verse 13 all the times God says, "If I." "*If I* shut up heaven …" "*If I* command the locusts …" "*If I* send pestilence …"

These verses are clearly telling us who is in control. God is. When we plead with God, we need to recognize who is in control and *believe* that He is our rescuer. God does not want us to blame everything on Satan. Satan has no more power than God allows. It is God who is in control here and He wants our attention on Him, and nowhere else.

When we recognize that God is in control and believe in Him to take care of all our trials, we humble ourselves, pray, earnestly seek His face, and turn from our wicked ways. This is a plea, a desperate cry for salvation from the drought, from the locusts that devour the land, from the pestilence among the people. It is a cry for help that must be answered and cannot go unheard lest we lose all hope. Then God will hear us from heaven, forgive us our sins, and heal our land.

Perhaps if we were to view the Christian life as a plea, or a series of pleas, we would begin to see changes in our lives, our land, and our world today.

ABOUT THE AUTHOR

Mr. Orman was born in May of 1961 near the Kennedy Space Center in Florida. Growing up in Florida he was exposed to science and technology at the Space Center, but also religion at Bible believing churches. Eventually, this would lead to him serving as Pastor at Nanakuli Baptist Church in Hawaii. He served in the United States Coast Guard, has 22 years of industry technology experience, and 16 years of U.S. Government experience with the DoD. Today, he and his wife are retired in Hawaii.

Printed in the United States
by Baker & Taylor Publisher Services